Cyberbullying

Abusive Relationships in Cyberspace

Editor:
Peter K. Smith

Zeitschrift für Psychologie
Journal of Psychology

Vol. 217, No. 4, 2009

Library of Congress Cataloging in Publication

is available via the Library of Congress Marc Database under the
LC Control Number 2009932408

Library and Archives Canada Cataloguing in Publication

Cyberbullying : abusive relationships in cyberspace / Peter K. Smith, editor.

Published as part of the journal Zeitschrift für Psychologie.

Includes bibliographical references.
ISBN 978-0-88937-379-2

1. Cyberbullying. I. Smith, Peter K II. Title: Zeitschrift für Psychologie.

HV6773.C92 2009 302.3 C2009-904512-5

PUBLISHING OFFICES
USA: Hogrefe Publishing, 875 Massachusetts Avenue, 7th Floor, Cambridge, MA 02139
Phone (866) 823-4726, Fax (617) 354-6875; E-mail customerservice@hogrefe-publishing.com
EUROPE: Hogrefe Publishing, Rohnsweg 25, 37085 Göttingen, Germany
Phone +49 551 49609-0, Fax +49 551 49609-88, E-mail publishing@hogrefe.com

SALES & DISTRIBUTION
USA: Hogrefe Publishing, Customer Services Department, 30 Amberwood Parkway, Ashland,
OH 44805, Phone (800) 228-3749, Fax (419) 281-6883, E-mail customerservice@hogrefe.com
EUROPE: Hogrefe Publishing, Rohnsweg 25, 37085 Göttingen, Germany
Phone +49 551 49609-0, Fax +49 551 49609-88, E-mail publishing@hogrefe.com

OTHER OFFICES
CANADA: Hogrefe Publishing, 660 Eglinton Ave. East, Suite 119-514, Toronto, Ontario M4G 2K2
SWITZERLAND: Hogrefe Publishing, Länggass-Strasse 76, CH-3000 Bern 9

Hogrefe Publishing
Incorporated and registered in the Commonwealth of Massachusetts, USA, and in Göttingen, Lower Saxony, Germany

ISBN 978-0-88937-379-2

Contents

A New Structure for the *Zeitschrift für Psychologie / Journal of Psychology*

More Information, More Communication!

Bernd Leplow

Institute of Psychology, University of Halle-Wittenberg, Halle, Germany

The ideal topical issue or monograph should be more than just a compilation of high-quality research papers. It should cover the broad range of aspects of the topic, including various standpoints, new developments, the activities of young or recently established research groups, as well as information on new books and papers or even relevant specialist conferences. The ideal topical issue also has to be compiled by a leading expert on the subject in question, and so generally it will be guest editors who are best qualified to do this under the "meta-guidance" of a team of editors.

It is for these reasons that we have decided to refine the structure of *Zeitschrift für Psychologie/Journal of Psychology* (ZfP/JoP), the second oldest psychology journal in the world, from this issue onwards. The journal will continue to consist entirely of topical issues. Each will now generally start with a *Review Article* or an *Editorial* covering the major aspects of the topic, followed by three to five high-quality *Research Papers* written by international experts. These "conventional" scientific papers will generally be supplemented by one or more *Research Spotlight* articles, allowing the guest editor to add information about promising work that is still ongoing at the time of publication, including (for instance) work that is of interest and note but that has not yet been developed to the point where a full original paper is warranted. *Opinion* pieces examining the pros and cons of scientific approaches, the significance of results or their consequences for society will be a further core element of the new *ZfP/JoP*. Finally, brief *Horizons* articles will inform readers about current activities related to the respective topic (i.e., conferences, meetings, new research programs, books, and announcements). The editors of the journal feel sure that this more up-to-date structure for a scientific journal will enhance its readability and, we hope, stimulate its acceptance and distribution.

To this end, the publisher is now producing the issues in a new and more attractive layout, with a more robust cover, and is giving the individual issues of *Zeitschrift für Psychologie/Journal of Psychology* an ISBN to make them available for purchase individually via any online or regular bookstore.

At this juncture I'd like to thank Peter Smith for doing the job of compiling the very first issue with the new features! He has put together an exciting issue about cyberbullying, containing not only a brief editorial review article about "Abusive Relationships in Cyberspace" written by himself and five original papers covering various aspects to the topic, but also using the Research Spotlight format for brief reports about the situation in Germany and the Czech Republic. Critical commentaries about measurement and definition of cyberbullying are outlined in an Opinion article. Finally, everybody who is interested in new programs and various other activities concerned with cyberbullying will be thankful for the five reports Peter Smith selected for the Horizons section.

It is the hope and the wish of the whole editorial team that the new structure for *ZfP/JoP*, along with the selection of topics alternating between basic research and more applied research, will help not only to contribute to scientific communication but also the transfer of scientific knowledge into society in general.

Bernd Leplow

Institute of Psychology
University of Halle-Wittenberg
Brandbergweg 23
D-06120 Halle
Germany
Tel. +49 345 552 4358/4359
Fax +49 345 552 7218
E-mail bernd.leplow@psych.uni-halle.de

DOI: 10.1027/0044-3409.217.4.179

Cyberbullying

Abusive Relationships in Cyberspace

Peter K. Smith

Psychology Department, Goldsmiths, University of London, UK

"Bullying" refers to abusive relationships, where there are repeated, intentionally hurtful actions directed against a victim (or victims) who is in a less powerful situation and thus not able to defend themselves effectively. It has been studied now for some 30 years (Olweus, 1978; Smith et al., 1999), especially among school pupils; but the abuse of power can always be a temptation, and bullying is found across age groups and in many contexts (Monks et al., 2009). It is known that forms of bullying can be physical, verbal, and psychological; direct and indirect.

Only this century however has a new major form of bullying become noticeable, often called cyberbullying. This encompasses bullying by mobile phones, and the Internet, in many different guises (e.g., text messages, video-clips, e-mails, websites, and virtual worlds). Cyberbullying has some similarities to traditional forms of bullying, but also important differences. It appears to be a growing phenomenon, with a need for research to help us understand the nature of cyberbullying, its effects, and ways of coping with it at an individual and institutional level. Fortunately, this research effort is growing rapidly, as this Special Issue helps to demonstrate.

Many psychological researchers in the area of what is now often called "traditional" bullying have moved into researching cyberbullying; plus, it has attracted new researchers, some from other disciplines such as information technology or legal studies (Shariff, 2008). Although research on traditional bullying originated in Europe, much early research on cyberbullying has come from the USA (Kowalski, Limber, & Agatston, 2008). However this area is already an international one (Li, Cross, & Smith, in press), with much happening in Europe (see the Research Activities entries, this issue; Katzer, 2009, for Germany).

Much of the work on cyberbullying focuses on school-aged children and young people, and indeed this does seem to be the age period where it is most prevalent (Sevcikova & Smahel, 2009). However, it also occurs in adult life, and beyond simple mobile phone and e-mail contexts. Coyne, Chesney, Logan, and Madden (2009) consider what is called "griefing" in virtual world communities.

The nature of the differences between cyberbullying and traditional bullying is intriguing, with the potential for giving insight into motivations for cyberbullying and relevant for intervention programs. This aspect underlies the first four articles in this Special Issue. Dooley, Pyżalski, and Cross (2009) consider some of these differences, relating to definitional issues such as repetition and power imbalance in the cyber context; they then venture into a discussion of social information processing factors that distinguish cyberbullying. Spears, Slee, Owens, and Johnson (2009) provide qualitative data that give us some further insights into aspects such as power imbalance and feelings of helplessness in victims. The emotional impact on victims of four types of bullying (two traditional and two cyber) is explored in detail by Ortega, Elipe, Mora-Merchán, Calmaestra, and Vega (2009). Gradinger, Strohmeier, and Spiel (2009) examine some risk factors for involvement in cyberbullying, as well as the overlap between traditional and cyberbullying and victimization; Schultze-Krumbholz and Scheithauer (2009) also examine some socio-emotional correlates of cyberbullying.

This new area of study raises important methodological issues, both definitional and measurement, two aspects that are clearly related. Menesini and Nocentini (2009) offer some thoughts on these matters. It is hoped that this Special Issue will give a flavor of the range of topics and methodologies being employed in this rather new area of study, and that it will provide a stimulus for further debate and help us to develop constructive strategies for dealing with what is likely to become an increasingly important social problem.

References

Coyne, I., Chesney, T., Logan, B., & Madden, N. (2009). Griefing in a virtual community: An exploratory survey of second life residents. *Zeitschrift für Psychologie / Journal of Psychology, 217*(4), 214–221.

Dooley, J. J., Pyżalski, J., & Cross, D. (2009). Cyberbullying versus face-to-face bullying: A theoretical and conceptual review. *Zeitschrift für Psychologie / Journal of Psychology, 217*(4), 182–188.

Gradinger, P., Strohmeier, D., & Spiel, C. (2009). Traditional bullying and cyberbullying identification of risk groups for adjustment problems. *Zeitschrift für Psychologie / Journal of Psychology, 217*(4), 205–213.

Katzer, C. (2009). Cyberbullying in Germany: What has been done and what is going on. *Zeitschrift für Psychologie / Journal of Psychology, 217*(4), 222–223.

DOI: 10.1027/0044-3409.217.4.180

Kowalski, R. M., Limber, S. P., & Agatston, P. W. (2008). *Cyber bullying: Bullying in the digital age*. Malden, MA: Blackwell Publishing.

Li, Q., Cross, D., & Smith, P. K. (Eds.). (in press). *Bullying in the global village*. Oxford: Wiley-Blackwell.

Menesini, E., & Nocentini, A. (2009). Cyberbullying definition and measurement: Some critical considerations. *Zeitschrift für Psychologie / Journal of Psychology, 217*(4), 230–232.

Monks, C. P., Smith, P. K., Naylor, P., Barter, C., Ireland, J. L., & Coyne, I. (2009). Bullying in different contexts: Commonalities, differences and the role of theory. *Aggression and Violent Behavior, 14*, 146–156.

Olweus, D. (1978). *Aggression in the schools: Bullies and whipping boys*. Washington, DC: Hemisphere.

Ortega, R., Elipe, P., Mora-Merchán, J. A., Calmaestra, J., & Vega, E. (2009). The emotional impact on victims of traditional bullying and cyberbullying: A study of Spanish adolescents. *Zeitschrift für Psychologie / Journal of Psychology, 217*(4), 197–204.

Schultze-Krumbholz, A., & Scheithauer, H. (2009). Social-behavioral correlates of cyberbullying in a German student sample. *Zeitschrift für Psychologie / Journal of Psychology, 217*(4), 224–226.

Sevcikova, A., & Smahel, D. (2009). Online harassment and cyberbullying in the Czech Republic: Comparison across age groups. *Zeitschrift für Psychologie / Journal of Psychology, 217*(4), 227–229.

Shariff, S. (2008). *Cyber-bullying: Issues and solutions for the school, the classroom and the home*. London and New York: Routledge.

Smith, P. K., Morita, Y., Junger-Tas, J., Olweus, D., Catalano, R., & Slee, P. (Eds.). (1999). *The nature of school bullying: A cross-national perspective*. London: Routledge.

Spears, B., Slee, P., Owens, L., & Johnson, B. (2009). Behind the scenes and screens insights into the human dimension of covert and cyberbullying. *Zeitschrift für Psychologie / Journal of Psychology, 217*(4), 189–196.

Peter K. Smith

Unit for School and Family Studies
Psychology Department
Goldsmiths
University of London
New Cross
London SE14 6NW
UK
Tel. +44 20 7919 7898
Fax +44 20 7919 7873
E-mail p.smith@gold.ac.uk

Cyberbullying Versus Face-to-Face Bullying

A Theoretical and Conceptual Review

Julian J. Dooley,[1] Jacek Pyżalski,[2,3] and Donna Cross[1]

[1]Child Health Promotion Research Centre, Edith Cowan University, Mt. Lawley, WA, Australia
[2]The Pedagogy Academy, Lodz, Poland
[3]Nofer Institute of Occupational Medicine, Lodz, Poland

Abstract. Cyberbullying has been described as a type of electronic bullying and has recently been subjected to intense media scrutiny largely due to a number of high profile and tragic cases of teen suicide. Despite the media attention relatively little is known about the nature of cyberbullying. This is, at least in part, due to a lack of theoretical and conceptual clarity and an examination of the similarities and differences between cyberbullying and face-to-face bullying. This paper reviews the limited theoretical and empirical literature addressing both cyberbullying and face-to-face bullying, using some specific examples from a qualitative study for illustration. We compare and contrast individual factors common to cyber and face-to-face bullying. We then examine social information processing factors associated with face-to-face bullying and present a discussion of the similarities and differences that may characterize cyberbullying.

Keywords: cyberbullying, face-to-face bullying, theory

To date cyberbullying has received significant media attention driven by some recent cases resulting in criminal or civil lawsuits filed against the perpetrator as well as, in some incidences, the school. Despite this attention, many questions about cyberbullying are yet to be answered. For example, is cyberbullying analogous to face-to-face bullying? Are cyberbullying and face-to-face bullying conceptually and theoretically similar? We review the cyberbullying literature, examining the conceptual and theoretical similarities and differences between cyberbullying and face-to-face bullying.

While this paper treats those who engage in cyberbullying or face-to-face bullying behaviors as two distinct groups, we acknowledge the evidence indicating the overlap between them (e.g., Raskauskas & Stoltz, 2007). However, to examine cyberbullying and face-to-face bullying it is necessary to describe and compare the "discrete" forms as distinct behaviors enacted by different people. This should not be interpreted as meaning that individuals cannot or do not engage in both forms of the behavior. This paper aims to start a dialog to improve our conceptual understanding of cyberbullying and henceforth approaches to measurement and the development of prevention/intervention strategies.

Given that the theoretical discourse regarding cyberbullying is limited, we draw on available empirical literature for illustration. In addition we use some qualitative data, collected by the second author via face-to-face interviews, e-interviews, and focus groups. Participants were Polish university students aged 12–25. The interviews and focus group sessions addressed: general use patterns of communication technologies and their role in daily life, the role of communication technologies in building and maintaining relationships, the bullying concepts of repetition of behaviors and imbalance of power, as well as experiences as a victim, perpetrator, or witness of cyberbullying. Quotations obtained during these sessions are used to illustrate examples of various aspects of bullying behaviors.

Definition

Bullying is usually defined as aggression that is intentionally carried out by one or more individuals and repeatedly targeted toward a person who cannot easily defend him- or herself (e.g., Olweus, 1993). Olweus identified two factors crucial to differentiating between aggression and bullying: aggression is a single act whereas bullying comprises repeated acts; and bully-victim relationships are characterized by an imbalance of power while aggression can be between two persons of equal power. Finally, including intentionality in the definition excludes acts bereft of malice.

To date, cyberbullying has been difficult to define and compare because, as Kowalski, Limber, and Agatston (2008) noted, the methods employed are varied. However, cyberbullying has generally been defined as bullying using an electronic medium, adopting the definition of Olweus, or something similar. Smith et al. (2008, p. 376) defined cyberbullying as "an aggressive, intentional act carried out by a group or individual, using electronic forms of contact, repeatedly and over time against a victim who cannot easily defend him or herself." Major components to this definition

Zeitschrift für Psychologie / Journal of Psychology 2009; Vol. 217(4):182–188
DOI: 10.1027/0044-3409.217.4.182

are that the act must be *aggressive*, *intentional*, *repetitive*, and with a *power imbalance*. Belsey (2004) defined cyberbullying as "the use of information and communication technologies to support deliberate, repeated, and hostile behavior by an individual or group that is intended to harm others." Note the absence of a power imbalance, suggesting that online power is not a necessary component. Alternatively, Wolak, Mitchell, and Finkelhor (2006, 2007) suggest that it is more accurate to consider repeated acts of online aggression as *online harassment*. Further, Wolak et al. (2006) argued that, as negative online interactions can be easily terminated, the victim is in a position of power they would not have if the bullying occurred in the schoolyard from which they cannot easily escape. However, Wolak et al. (2007) note that there are instances of online victimization that cannot be easily terminated, such as the difficulties associated with removing information (e.g., on websites) from the Internet.

To proceed with uniformity the core components of cyberbullying must be identified. Vandebosch and van Cleemput (2008) conducted focus groups with 10–19 year olds in Belgium about their experiences with information and communication technology (ICT) and cyberbullying. These data suggested that cyberbullying behavior must be intentional, repetitive, and characterized by a power imbalance – the same factors considered central to face-to-face bullying, and suggested that the behavior not the medium is important. Similarly, Kowalski et al. (2008) suggested that cyberbullying is the electronic form of face-to-face bullying rather than a distinct phenomenon. However, considering cyberbullying as merely the electronic form of face-to-face bullying may overlook intricacies of these behaviors. As bullying (and cyberbullying) behaviors are, by almost all definitions, intentionally hurtful, the next section will focus on the more contentious issues of repetition and power imbalance.

Repetition

Olweus (1993) argued that repetition is necessary in the definition of bullying, in order to exclude occasional acts of aggression directed at different people at different times. Nonetheless, it is feasible that multiple acts of aggression by a single person toward numerous individuals may be considered bullying independent of whether the person being aggressed is considered a victim of bullying. The repetitive nature of the aggressive behavior can be used to instill fear, thus causing psychological harm to a victim. As bullying behaviors take many forms (e.g., physical hitting and gossiping) it is argued that it is the repetitive nature of acts intended to harm that is crucial and not necessarily the nature of the behavior itself.

Although the inclusion of repetition in the definition is generally accepted, debate continues about its nature and importance. For example, Tattum (1989) argued that ongoing feelings of stress about an incident may be considered repetitive even though the act occurred only once. Similarly, Guerin and Hennessy (2002) found that over 50% of their sample of children did not consider the frequency of occurrence to be important, with over 40% of those believing that an act that occurred once or twice could still be bullying.

Repetition in cyberbullying is especially problematic to operationalize, as there can be differences between the perpetrator and victim in terms of perceptions of how many incidences occur and the potential consequences. While repetition is clear when a perpetrator sends numerous phone text messages or e-mails (e.g., Slonje & Smith, 2008), it is not so clear when a bully creates a single derogatory website, or a message on a website, which many people can access (Leishman, 2005). A single aggressive act such as uploading an embarrassing picture to the Internet can result in continued and widespread ridicule and humiliation for the victim. Whereas the aggressive act is not repeated the damage caused by the act is relived through the ongoing humiliation.

If it is assumed that not all forms of cyberbullying are equal in terms of victim impact (Smith et al., 2008), such that the effect of receiving a threatening text message is not the same as receiving a threatening message in an online chatroom, then it follows that some acts may not need to be repeated (or repeated as often) to inflict harm. Further, Vandebosch and van Cleemput (2008) noted that a single cyber act could be sufficient to be considered bullying, especially if this act followed on from a series of offline acts of bullying. Along these lines, Fauman (2008) suggested that as information posted online can be widely disseminated, the repetitive nature of the act by the person bullying may not be as important as in face-to-face bullying.

The relative permanence of pictures or videos posted online for anyone to view is likely to have a similar effect (or possibly worse) than an offline act. Having an embarrassing picture posted on the Internet has the potential for significant and long-lasting social and emotional harm. This is illustrated in an interview with a 22-year-old girl whose drunk behavior at a party was video recorded and then posted on the Internet. She reported feeling like the act was being repeated as she watched the number of website hits increase. Slonje and Smith (2008) found that cyberbullying using picture/video clips was perceived by students as being more severe than other forms of cyberbullying primarily due to the large potential audience and because they can be identified. Therefore, it appears that the damage experienced in cyberbullying may be largely social and emotional in nature and is exacerbated by the potential scale of the damage inflicted.

Power Imbalance

An imbalance in power between perpetrator and victim has been described as a fundamental aspect of bullying that permits the distinction between acts of aggression and bullying. Aalsma and Brown (2008) use the example of a sixth grade boy being kicked on the bus every day by a smaller, emotionally impaired second grader suggesting that bullying did not occur because the second grade child was smaller (and less physically powerful) than the sixth grade child. However, implicit in their example is that a sixth grader should not be afraid of a smaller second grader which, of course, is not necessarily always the case. The assessment of power imbalance is complicated because it is difficult to assess, especially in younger populations (Mishna, 2004, 2006). The issue of power is further complicated as power can be social, psychological, or physical in nature (Monks & Smith, 2006). Olweus (1997) has made reference to the "weak" victim, meaning not merely physically weak but also mentally weak. The acknowledgment that aggression (and bullying) can be enacted to damage a person's social and relational status indicates that power can come in many forms. In fact, Rigby (2007, p. 19) noted that "wherever there is a power imbalance, whatever its source, an individual can be reduced in status."

Conceptualizing and assessing power imbalance in cyber-based interactions is even more complicated than in traditional forms of bullying. With Rigby's comment in mind, power in online relationships can be interpreted as more advanced technological skills. However, it does not require an advanced skill set to take a picture using a mobile phone camera and send it to others. Similarly, posting a picture online or creating a fake social network site profile requires only a basic skill set. Other more complicated forms of cyberbullying (e.g., manipulating and modifying pictures) require more advanced skills but these forms are relatively less common (Smith et al., 2008).

It has been suggested that one of the distinguishing features of cyberbullying is the inability of victims to get away from it (Slonje & Smith, 2008). Unlike with face-to-face bullying, there is potentially no reprise from technology-based interactions as they can be received at any time of the day or night. In this sense, the inability to have any control over acts of bullying may result in feelings of powerlessness in the person being bullied.

To date, few have explicitly measured the nature of power imbalance in online interactions. Vandebosch and van Cleemput (2008) reported that those who engaged in cyberbullying behaviors acknowledged that many of/most of their victims knew them in the real world (although the perpetrators concealed their identity) and that the victims were perceived as being of more, less, or equal strength. Interestingly, students in this study indicated that the weaker victims were also often the victims of face-to-face bullying whereas those considered more powerful in the real world were bullied due to the anonymity that ICT affords. More importantly, cybervictims reported that not knowing the identity of the bully increased feelings of frustration and powerlessness. Consistent with this, Fauman (2008) suggested that the ability to remain anonymous may minimize the necessity for those who bully to be more powerful than victims.

Given that most victims are cyberbullied by either another student at school or a stranger (Kowalski & Limber, 2007) the anonymity afforded to perpetrators is an important issue. Smith et al. (2008) reported from focus groups that students believed phone text messaging was the most common form of cyberbullying as it enabled those who bully to remain anonymous. Consistent with this, we noted a male participant (17 years old) in a focus group, who encouraged his peers to send threatening phone text messages from many unknown numbers, openly expressed such awareness by commenting that the victim "is in real trouble ... he doesn't know who is sending this – doesn't know what can happen – it's better when he's uncertain what can happen..." Similarly, in a face-to-face interview a 15-year-old girl described receiving a series of anonymous phone text messages criticizing her harshly. She reported that it was not the content of messages but the anonymity of the author that was the most threatening. Anonymity appears to be an important feature of cyberbullying for perpetrators who report that they would not engage in offline bullying (Vandebosch & van Cleemput, 2008). This highlights the potential for growth in cyberbullying, given that many more people could engage in this behavior than would normally engage in face-to-face bullying.

Table 1 outlines how the two primary constructs (imbalance of power and repetition) relate to face-to-face and cyberbullying contexts. The relationship between anonymity and power in cyberbullying behavior has yet to be thoroughly addressed and may reveal important differences between cyber- and face-to-face bullying, especially in relation to how information is processed in cyberbullying interactions. Before addressing the information processing patterns that characterize bullying behaviors, we examine if bullying presents in different forms which will further enable the identification of cognitive motivations that characterize these forms.

Table 1. The constructs of imbalance of power, and repetition, in relation to face-to-face and cyberbullying

	Face-to-face bullying	Cyberbullying
Imbalance of power	Usually connected to the features of perpetrators and their relative physical and/or psychological power in a real world	May be related to the features of perpetrators, but often to "a power of technology" and the features of the content published on the Internet or features of computer mediated communication (e.g., anonymity)
		May be based on a victim's lack of power as opposed to a perpetrator's possession of power
Repetition	Based on behavioral repetition over time conducted by perpetrators	May be based on technology and the specific features of the content published – not initial perpetrator's intentions and behavior

Forms of Bullying

Early researchers primarily focused on physical and verbal aggression that characterized bullying interactions. In the 1990s researchers recognized that other more subtle forms of aggression were also being used, such as relational aggression, characterized by attempts or threats to damage relationships (e.g., Crick & Grotpeter, 1996). Relational aggression consists of subtle behaviors (e.g., gossiping) which are more frequently observed in women (Coyne, Archer, & Eslea, 2006). Underwood (2003) also described social aggression, which was a broader form of aggression than relational aggression, where many tactics were employed in an attempt to destroy all types of social relationships as well as a person's self-esteem and social status.

These forms of aggression can be either direct or indirect in how they are enacted (e.g., Björkqvist, Österman, & Kaukiainen, 1992). For example, direct forms would include telling someone they cannot join in a game or by being verbally aggressive whereas indirect forms would include gossiping or spreading nasty rumors. The primary difference is that direct aggression is enacted directly toward the victim (so the victim is aware who the aggressor is) while indirect aggression is directed at the victim via a third (or more) party so it is not always possible to identify the aggressor (i.e., the person who started the rumor). Additionally, bullying has also been described in terms of reactive (i.e., emotionally volatile and explosive) versus proactive (i.e., planned and controlled aggression designed to dominate others or to acquire tangible objects such as lunch money). To date, much research has focused on the reactive/proactive aggression dichotomy especially in relation to the cognitive motivations that drive these forms of aggression (e.g., Fontaine, 2007).

Smith et al. (2008) described seven modes of cyberbullying: phone call, mobile phone text messaging, e-mail, picture/video clip, instant messaging, website, and chatroom. Clearly, there are distinct differences between some of these media in terms of the nature of contact between the bully and the victim (e.g., phone call requires the bully to speak to the victim while e-mail requires no "direct" contact) as well as the level of technological skills required (e.g., the skills required to set up a website are more complex than the skills required to send a mobile phone text message). Smith and colleagues (Slonje & Smith, 2008; Smith et al., 2008) demonstrated the differential impact of each of these types of cyberbullying in comparison with face-to-face bullying. In general, the impact of picture/video clip bullying was considered worse than face-to-face bullying, while the impact of phone call and text messaging bullying (Smith et al., 2008) or of text message and e-mail bullying (Slonje & Smith, 2008) was considered better (i.e., less damaging) than face-to-face bullying. Clearly, the different types of cyberbullying are not equal in terms of the skills needed to engage in the behavior as well as the impact they have on victims. It would be interesting to determine if there is an association between a perpetrator's motivation (e.g., revenge vs. fun) and the type of media used to cyberbully.

Although both the mobile phone and Internet lend themselves to verbal threats and insults the anonymity afforded by these forms of cyberbullying makes the classification more complex. For example, it is possible to directly aggress toward a person in an online chatroom or via text message (i.e., being verbally aggressive) but this could be considered indirect aggression as the identity of the perpetrator is concealed. Therefore, the same act of aggression can have both direct and indirect components to it. In relation to proactive aggression, the use of aggression is considered a means of interpersonal dominance (i.e., getting others to do what you want them to) or of object acquisition (Pepler, Jiang, Craig, & Connolly, 2008). This type of aggression has often been associated with bullying, especially in relation to its instrumental motives (see Fontaine, 2007, for a detailed discussion of the differences between proactive/instrumental and reactive aggression).

Although the literature is sparse it can be concluded that the motives for engaging in these acts of aggression are primarily focused on inflicting harm and fear. Vandebosch and van Cleemput (2008) reported that students indicated that revenge for being bullied in real life was a primary motivation for some. Similarly, Raskauskas and Stoltz (2007, p. 570) found that 25% of those who cyberbullied others engaged in aggressive behaviors to "get back at someone they're mad at." For others, cyberbullying was in reaction to a previous argument or was a means for the person bullying to display their technological skills; and almost 40% of those who cyberbullied others reported engaging in online aggression for fun. Given this, it is highly likely, as suggested by Slonje and Smith (2008), that not having to see the fear in a victim's eyes and being less aware of the consequences reduces the potential for empathy and remorse – factors which would lessen the likelihood of future acts of aggression and bullying. However, these reasons offer only anecdotal evidence and, to date, no studies have thoroughly assessed the motivation that drives cyberbullying and whether it is different than for face-to-face bullying. One method of understanding the motivations for bullying behaviors is to examine the patterns of information processing associated with these behaviors.

Information Processing and Bullying

A number of theoretical models have been proposed to describe and explain the processing of social information that drives aggressive and bullying behaviors. To date, the most empirically supported model was proposed by Crick and Dodge (1994). The social information processing (SIP) model describes five interrelated cognitive processes believed to underlie social behaviors: (1) internal and external stimuli are encoded; (2) encoded information is interpreted and attributions of intent and causality are made; (3) a social goal is generated; (4) responses are generated that will lead to its attainment; and (5) the response that is attributed the highest overall value is chosen (Fontaine & Dodge, 2006). In terms of aggression research, the stages of attribution (Stage 2) and response decision (Stage 5) are the most frequently addressed.

One of the most consistent findings in the SIP and aggression literature is the association between reactive aggression and the tendency toward attributing hostile intent in ambiguous social interactions (e.g., Crick & Dodge, 1996; Hartman & Stage, 2000; Orobio de Castro, Veerman, Koops, Bosch, & Monshouwer, 2002). Unlike reactive aggression, proactive aggression has been associated with differences in latter stages of the SIP model. The most consistent finding is the association between proactive aggression and the response decision stage of the SIP model (e.g., Crick & Dodge, 1996; Schwartz et al., 1998). For example, Crick and Dodge (1996) reported that proactively aggressive children were more likely to anticipate positive outcomes for their aggressive behavior. Similarly, Schwartz et al. (1998) reported that high rates of proactive aggression were associated with positive outcome expectancies for aggressive behavior. Thus, examining the patterns in which information is processed during social interactions has provided a means to distinguish between different forms of aggressive behavior and has provided important insights into the cognitive motivations that drive these behaviors (e.g., Camodeca & Goossens, 2005).

To date, no studies have examined SIP in relation to cyberbullying. We are not suggesting that the patterns of information processing associated with cyberbullying behavior will be totally distinct from what has been reported in relation to, for example, proactive aggression. However, given the media typically used to engage in cyberbullying and that those who engage in cyberbullying behaviors do not necessarily engage in face-to-face bullying, we suggest there may be some subtle differences between how information is processed in these interactions. For example, the expectation of positive outcomes after aggressive behavior (a finding primarily related to those who bully either getting people to do what they want or acquiring an object) may be the same for the cyberbully but, importantly, the goal toward which the behavior is directed may differ. If, as was suggested by Vandebosch and van Cleemput (2008), those who cyberbully others are more motivated by revenge then the explicit goal is to hurt rather than to dominate or to acquire.

However, due to the nature of the medium in which cyberbullying is enacted, those who bully are no longer reinforced for their behavior in the traditional manner. For example, if a person engaging in face-to-face bullying behaviors is motivated (and goal oriented) to inflict harm primarily using fear, then they will likely be reinforced for this behavior by the body language and facial expression (as well as the verbal response) of their victim. The reinforcement is immediate and tangible. In contrast, a person engaging in cyberbullying behaviors who is motivated to socially hurt others may have to wait for a period of time before the impact is apparent (at least until the text message, picture, or other material is distributed among the group).

Similarly, the person engaging in cyberbullying behaviors who is motivated to inflict harm using fear has limited external sources of reinforcement and may have to, at least initially, rely on their own reactions to their acts. The reward for engaging in some forms of cyberbullying could be based to a larger extent on the expectations the person engaging in bullying behaviors has for how the target person *will* react versus how the target person *is* reacting, than is the case with face-to-face bullying. This delay between the act (i.e., creating a fake website) and the outcome (i.e., sharing secrets with the school) would likely result in a heightened sense of expectation and a built-up level of excitement and anticipation for the time when the target person realizes what has been done. Thus, it is feasible that a difference exists between those engaging in cyberbullying behaviors versus face-to-face bullying behaviors according to the generation of goals and the expectations related to the outcome of an interaction. It may be the case that these differences are only observed in relation to different types of cyberbullying.

Gender Differences

One of the most interesting aspects of the bullying/cyberbullying debate relates to gender differences in the rates of these behaviors. Traditionally, men engage in more bullying behaviors than women (Forero, McLellan, Rissel, & Baum, 1999; Nansel et al., 2001; Sourander, Helstela, Helenius, & Piha, 2000). However, Blair (2003) reported that women are more likely to communicate using text messaging and e-mail than are men; this, combined with the more covert (and social) nature of cyberbullying, would make it reasonable to expect that the gender differences demonstrated in face-to-face bullying are, at the least, not as strong in cyberbullying. Indeed, some have reported that men and women were equally likely to report harassing others online (Williams & Guerra, 2007; Ybarra & Mitchell, 2004). Similarly, Slonje and Smith (2008) reported no gender differences in the self-reported rates of being either engaging in or being the target of cyberbullying behaviors (a trend suggesting boys engaged in more acts of cyberbullying than girls was not statistically significant). In contrast, Li (2006) reported that men were more likely to engage in cyberbullying behaviors than their female counterparts. Although these results do not suggest that women engage in more cyberbullying than men they do indicate that the gender differences reported in relation to face-to-face bullying are not as strong. Further, girls tend to have more close-knit relationships/friendships and therefore more readily exchange intimate details and personal secrets whereas boys socialize in larger groups and share fewer details. That girls use text messaging and e-mail more than boys may result in more opportunities to spread secrets and have their secrets spread online.

Group Effect

It has been noted that one of the most distressing aspects of traditional face-to-face bullying is the effect of the group, an effect which perpetuates and sustains the abuse of the target of the bullying behaviors (Bukowski & Sippola, 2001; Crick, Grotpeter, & Bigbee, 2002; Salmivalli, 2001). Sutton, Smith, and Swettenham (1999) cautioned against overlooking the importance of the group and social aspects of bullying over and above the internal cognitive processing patterns that characterize other forms of aggression (i.e., hostile attribution of intent patterns observed in reactively aggressive individuals; Orobio de Castro et al., 2002). Further, Shariff (2008) commented that the need for power and recognition in those who bully is satisfied by the recruitment of others in the victimization of an individual. Support for this can be found in the research examining the effect of proactive aggression (the type of aggression considered typical of bullying interactions). Proactively aggressive children are seen as positive leaders with a good sense of humor, high self-esteem qualities and positive early friendship qualities, and high social status (Dodge & Coie, 1987).

This aspect of face-to-face bullying may have significant similarities with cyberbullying in that the bullying behavior (e.g., taking an embarrassing picture) becomes much more serious when viewed by a large group of schoolchildren. In fact, given how quickly and extensively images can be distributed to groups using mobile phones or the Internet, it is not surprising that the effect of such an act would be more distressing and damaging to a victim than being bullied in a face-to-face interaction which only a small group of individuals would observe. In essence, the effect of the cyber group far surpasses the schoolyard group given that the former is not bound by the school walls and the potential audience is limitless.

Conclusion

Cyberbullying comprises a set of aggressive behaviors that are enacted via electronic media. This is a relatively new form of bullying that is receiving more and more attention in the research literature. Relatively little is still known about some aspects of cyberbullying, for example, the motivations and goals of those who cyberbully, the long-term impact of being cyberbullied, and the extent of the differences between cyberbullying and face-to-face bullying. This in turn makes it difficult to develop interventions to address this behavior with students who bully. As outlined above, several definitions of cyberbullying have been proposed, primarily based on the concept of face-to-face bullying. However, to date, there has been little or no discussion of the theoretical construct of cyberbullying and whether using electronic media to engage in acts of aggression is the same (or very similar) to engaging in aggressive acts in face-to-face interactions. In addition, to date no research has examined the nature of how information is processed in cyber interactions. Given that a large amount of cyberbullying is text based (i.e., sending text messages or e-mails), how this information is processed and how this differs from processing information in real-time social interactions are unclear. The reward for engaging in cyberbullying is often delayed (in contrast to face-to-face interactions), and this is anticipated to have an effect on how goals for these aggressive interactions are formed and pursued. With the increasing availability, use and reliance on electronic technology, the issues outlined here are going to become more important and are clearly worthy of far greater understanding. There is a clear need for further in-depth research addressing issues of power, motivation, and repetition in cyberbullying episodes.

Acknowledgment

The qualitative data described in this article were collected by Dr. Pyżalski as part of research funded by the Polish Ministry of Science and Higher Education, Grant No. 106 067735.

References

Aalsma, M. C., & Brown, J. R. (2008). What is bullying? *Journal of Adolescent Health, 43*, 101–102.

Belsey, B. (2004). *2004-07-15.* Available from www.cyberbullying.ca.

Björkqvist, K., Österman, K., & Kaukiainen, A. (1992). New trends in the study of female aggression. In K. Bjorkqvist & P. Niemelä (Eds.), *Of mice and women: Aspects of female aggression* (pp. 3–16). San Diego, CA: Academic Press.

Blair, J. (2003). New breed of bullies torment their peers on the Internet. *Education Week, 22*, 6–7.

Bukowski, W., & Sippola, L. (2001). Groups, individuals, and victimization: A view of the peer system. In J. Juvonen & S. Graham (Eds.), *Peer harassment in school: The plight of the vulnerable and victimized* (pp. 355–377). New York, NY: Guilford Press.

Camodeca, M., & Goossens, F. A. (2005). Aggression, social cognitions, anger and sadness in bullies and victims. *Journal of Child Psychology and Psychiatry, 46*, 185–197.

Coyne, S. M., Archer, J., & Eslea, M. (2006). "We're Not Friends Anymore! Unless...": The frequency and harmfulness of indirect, relational, and social aggression. *Aggressive Behavior, 32*, 294–307.

Crick, N. R., & Dodge, K. A. (1994). A review and reformulation of social information-processing mechanisms in children's social adjustment. *Psychological Bulletin, 115*, 74–101.

Crick, N. R., & Dodge, K. A. (1996). Social information-processing mechanisms in reactive and proactive aggression. *Child Development, 67*, 993–1002.

Crick, N. R., & Grotpeter, J. K. (1996). Children's treatment by peers: Victims of relational and overt aggression. *Development and Psychopathology, 8*, 367–380.

Crick, N. R., Grotpeter, J. K., & Bigbee, M. A. (2002). Relationally and physically aggressive children's intent attributions and feelings of distress for relational and instrumental peer provocations. *Child Development, 73*, 1134–1142.

Dodge, K. A., & Coie, J. D. (1987). Social-information-processing factors in reactive and proactive aggression in children's peer groups. *Journal of Personality and Social Psychology, 53*, 1146–1158.

Fauman, M. A. (2008). Cyber-bullying: Bullying in the digital age (book review). *The American Journal of Psychiatry, 165*, 780–781.

Fontaine, R. G. (2007). Disentangling the psychology and law of instrumental and reactive subtypes of aggression. *Psychology, Public Policy, and Law, 13*, 143–165.

Fontaine, R. G., & Dodge, K. A. (2006). Real-time decision making and aggressive behavior in youth: A heuristic model of response evaluation and decision (RED). *Aggressive Behavior, 32*, 604–624.

Forero, R., McLellan, L., Rissel, C., & Baum, A. (1999). Bullying behavior and psychosocial health among school students in New South Wales, Australia. *British Medical Journal, 319*, 344–348.

Guerin, S., & Hennessy, E. (2002). Pupils' definitions of bullying. *European Journal of Psychology of Education, 17*, 249–261.

Hartman, R., & Stage, S. A. (2000). The relationship between social information processing and in-school suspension for students with behavioral disorders. *Behavioral Disorders, 25*, 183–195.

Kowalski, R. M., & Limber, S. P. (2007). Electronic bullying among middle school students. *Journal of Adolescent Health, 41*, S22–S30.

Kowalski, R. M., Limber, S. P., & Agatston, P. W. (2008). *Cyber bullying*. Malden, MA: Blackwell.

Leishman, J. (2005). *Cyber-bullying* CBC News Online. Retrieved 27 November, 2008, from http://www.cbc.ca/news/background/bullying/cyber_bullying.html.

Li, Q. (2006). Cyberbullying in schools: A research of gender differences. *School Psychology International, 27*, 157–170.

Mishna, F. (2004). A qualitative study of bullying from multiple perspectives. *Child Schools, 26*, 234–247.

Mishna, F. (2006). Factors associated with perceptions and responses to bullying situations by children, parents, teachers and principals. *Victims and Offenders, 1*, 255–288.

Monks, C. P., & Smith, P. K. (2006). Definitions of bullying: Age differences in understanding of the term, and the role of experience. *British Journal of Developmental Psychology, 24*, 801–821.

Nansel, T. R., Overpeck, M., Pilla, R. S., Ruan, W. J., Simons-Morton, B., & Scheidt, P. (2001). Bullying behaviors among US youth: Prevalence and association with psychological adjustment. *Journal of the American Medical Association, 285*, 2094–2100.

Olweus, D. (1993). *Bullying at school: What we know and what we can do*. Cambridge, MA: Blackwell.

Olweus, D. (1997). Bully/victim problems in school: Facts and intervention. *European Journal of Psychology of Education, 12*, 495–510.

Orobio de Castro, B., Veerman, J. W., Koops, W., Bosch, J. D., & Monshouwer, H. J. (2002). Hostile attribution of intent and aggressive behavior: A meta-analysis. *Child Development, 73*, 916–934.

Pepler, D., Jiang, D., Craig, W., & Connolly, J. (2008). Developmental trajectories of bullying and associated factors. *Child Development, 79*, 325–338.

Raskauskas, J., & Stoltz, A. D. (2007). Involvement in traditional and electronic bullying among adolescents. *Developmental Psychology, 43*, 564–575.

Rigby, K. (2007). *Bullying in schools: And what to do about it*. Camberwell, Victoria: ACER.

Salmivalli, C. (2001). Group view on victimization: Empirical findings and their implications. In J. Juvonen & S. Graham (Eds.), *Peer harassment in school: The plight of the vulnerable and victimized* (pp. 398–419). New York, NY: Guilford.

Schwartz, D., Dodge, K. A., Coie, J. D., Hubbard, J. A., Cillessen, A. H. N., Lemerise, E. A., & Bateman, H. (1998). Socialcognitive and behavioral correlates of aggression and victimization in boys' play groups. *Journal of Abnormal Child Psychology, 26*(6), 431–440.

Shariff, S. (2008). *Cyber-bullying: Issues and solutions for the school the classroom and the home*. London: Routledge.

Slonje, R., & Smith, P. K. (2008). Cyberbullying: Another main type of bullying? *Scandinavian Journal of Psychology, 49*, 147–154.

Smith, P. K., Mahdavi, J., Carvalho, M., Fisher, S., Russell, S., & Tippett, N. (2008). Cyberbullying: Its nature and impact in secondary school pupils. *Journal of Child Psychology and Psychiatry, 49*, 376–385.

Sourander, A., Helstela, L., Helenius, H., & Piha, J. (2000). Persistence of bullying from childhood to adolescence: A longitudinal 8-year follow-up study. *Child Abuse and Neglect, 24*, 873–881.

Sutton, J., Smith, P. K., & Swettenham, J. (1999). Social cognition and bullying: Social inadequacy or skilled manipulation. *British Journal of Developmental Psychology, 17*, 435–450.

Tattum, D. P. (1989). Violence and aggression in schools. In D. P. Tattum & D. A. Lane (Eds.), *Bullying in school* (pp. 7–19). Stoke-on-Trent: Trentham Books.

Underwood, M. K. (2003). *Social aggression among girls*. New York, NY: Guilford.

Vandebosch, H., & van Cleemput, K. (2008). Defining cyberbullying: A qualitative research into the perceptions of youngsters. *CyberPsychology & Behavior, 11*, 499–503.

Williams, K. R., & Guerra, N. G. (2007). Prevalence and predictors of internet bullying. *Journal of Adolescent Health, 41*, S14–S21.

Wolak, J., Mitchell, K., & Finkelhor, D. (2006). *Online victimization: 5 years later*. Alexandria, VA: National Center for Missing & Exploited Children.

Wolak, J., Mitchell, K. J., & Finkelhor, D. (2007). Does online harassment constitute bullying? An exploration of online harassment by known peers and online-only contacts. *Journal of Adolescent Health, 41*, S51–S58.

Ybarra, M. L., & Mitchell, K. J. K. (2004). Youth engaging in online harassment: Associations with caregiver-child relationships, Internet use, and personal characteristics. *Journal of Adolescence, 27*, 319–336.

Julian J. Dooley

Child Health Promotion Research Centre
Edith Cowan University
Room 18.204
2 Bradford Street
Mt. Lawley
WA 6050
Australia
Tel. +61 8 9370 6101
Fax +61 8 9370 6511
E-mail j.dooley@ecu.edu.au

Behind the Scenes and Screens

Insights into the Human Dimension of Covert and Cyberbullying

Barbara Spears,[1] Phillip Slee,[2] Larry Owens,[2] and Bruce Johnson[1]

[1]University of South Australia, Magill, SA, Australia
[2]Flinders University, Adelaide, SA, Australia

Abstract. This qualitative study explores the human dimension of two subtypes of bullying in an Australian schooling context. Individuals' knowledge, understanding, and experiences of covert (*behind the scenes*) and cyber (*behind the screens*) bullying were explored through stories of what has actually been occurring in and around their schools. Participants were adolescent students (n = 20), teachers (n = 10) and school counselors (n = 6) from a variety of schools across Adelaide, South Australia. They recounted stories about covert and cyberbullying from their social networks and schooling contexts, giving authentic "voice" to these behaviors. Each narrative was uploaded to a dedicated website, contributing to an online "storybook," and providing information rich cases that enabled "issues of central importance" (Patton, 1987) to emerge. Narrative and thematic analyses revealed that covert and cyberbullying have much in common, but that cyberbullying in particular evoked strong negative feelings and emotions which included fear, as well as disruption to and dislocation from the participants' relationships. Participants indicated that the power differential was clearly understood and there was a clear sense of helplessness associated with cyberbullying. In particular, cyberbullying was found to operate both covertly and overtly via e-technologies, across school and home boundaries.

Keywords: bullying, covert, cyber, narrative inquiry, technology

While much is now known about the nature, prevalence, and impact of conventional bullying that occurs "offline" in school settings, research is only beginning to help us understand "online" bullying. There has been a dramatic rise in reports in the last 5 years referring to the use of communication media to intimidate, control, manipulate, put down, and humiliate others, with suggestions that this form of bullying may have greater impact than conventional bullying because it can occur at anytime (Hinduja & Patchin, 2008; Smith et al., 2008; Willard, 2007a, 2007b; Wolak, Mitchell, & Finkelhor, 2007). Many of these studies have sought to identify the behaviors employed and to determine the extent of cyberbullying, yet without an agreed upon definition, or consistent measures, comparison of studies remains difficult (Palfrey, 2008). In order to understand what is occurring in school contexts, there is a place for qualitative research, which seeks stakeholders' perspectives, experiences, and knowledge of this relatively recent phenomenon. These voices will contribute to what is already known from the prevalence studies, by adding a human dimension to the data: Authentic narratives and stories from the schooling sector which will reveal the lived experiences of impact and understanding of the nature of covert and cyberbullying.

Covert Bullying and Its Relationship to Cyberbullying

Unlike cyberbullying, the term covert bullying is not clearly defined in the literature, yet it is a term that is often used to loosely describe those behaviors which are less obvious and are more difficult to ascribe to any one in particular. In the absence of an agreed definition, covert bullying is defined here, as: *Typically repeated behaviors which are concealed, secret or clandestine, that inflict psychological/emotional harm through indirect/relational/social means where the target feels helpless and unable to retaliate.* It is used as an overarching behavioral descriptor: Often simply as the antonym of "overt" behaviors. While overt/covert are discrete subcategories, representing distinct opposites, covert bullying is rarely employed as an operational research term in its own right. Being synonymous with such terms as: secretive, clandestine, stealthy, underground, concealed, and hidden (online thesaurus) covert bullying encapsulates those "behind the scenes" behaviors which are often referred to as: *indirect*, *relational,* and *social* subtypes of aggression and bullying (see Archer & Coyne, 2005, for a review). Cyberbullying, however, occurs "behind the *screens*." If *cyber*bullying is viewed through the above

DOI: 10.1027/0044-3409.217.4.189

definition, it is apparent that it has distinct elements of covert bullying. Through the advent of e-technologies, *covert* bullying behaviors appear to have shifted to the cyber world, particularly when identity is suppressed or someone else's identity is assumed in order to inflict repeated harm on a target who is unable to respond. Online slam books and anonymous voting/polling booths, for example, are cyber-extensions of derogatory notes that would have previously been covertly passed around in class.

Measurement and Definitional Issues

Palfrey (2008) reported that there is difficulty in measuring online harassment and cyberbullying because there is no clear and consistent definition. The origin of the term cyberbullying is most often attributed to Canadian Bill Belsey; however Shariff (2008, p. 29) suggests that it is not entirely clear when the term came into common usage. What is evident is that as technologies have shifted in concert with Web 1.0 (pre-2004) to Web 2.0 (post-2004) environments, the definitions have come to reflect not only bullying in a cyber environment, but also the increasing sophistication of the technologies in use. Smith et al. (2008) captured the necessary components of the conventional bullying definition: A power imbalance and repetition and a deliberate intent to harm (Olweus, 1993), when defining cyberbullying as an "aggressive, intentional act carried out by a group or individual, using electronic forms of contact, repeatedly and over time against a victim who cannot easily defend him or herself." Belsey's current website (n.d.) (http://www.cyberbullying.ca) defines cyberbullying as "involving the use of information and communication technologies to support deliberate, repeated, and hostile behaviour by an individual or group, that is intended to harm others." Earlier definitions reflected the text-based technologies in use at that time: Willard (2003, cited in Shariff, 2008) referred to cyberbullying as "[on-line] *speech* that is defamatory, constitutes bullying, harassment or discrimination, discloses personal information or contains offensive, vulgar or defamatory comments." Patchin and Hinduja (2006) also suggested it is "wilful and repeated harm inflicted through the medium of *electronic text.*" The advent of cameras in mobile phones and the ability to upload them to social networking sites make the idea that cyberbullying is solely "speech" or "text" somewhat simplistic when considered alongside Internet ready mobile phones. What is evident is that as new technologies emerge and Web 3.0 evolves, the definition of cyberbullying will need to be continually revisited.

Impact

A survey involving 432 students from Alberta (Canada) indicated that more than half of cyber victims (57%) felt angry on numerous occasions and about one third (37%) felt sad and hurt (Beran & Li, 2007); see also Ortega, Elipe, Mora-Merchán, Calmaestra, and Vega (2009).

Earlier studies suggested that the impact of cyberbullying may be greater than for traditional bullying because it can occur at anytime and anywhere (Belsey, 2005). In addition, cyberbullies can more readily conceal their identity in cyberspace than they could in the "real world," contributing further to the possible impact of this form of bullying. Bullying via e-technology has meant that bullying has shifted from being "behind the scenes," where a conspiracy of silence often kept it removed from teachers' view, and where much bullying was covert and subtle, to "behind the screens" where identity can be hidden and where the acts of bullying appear in different forms via e-technologies, available to millions rather than a select few: for example, as text messages, video clips, e-mails, websites, or virtual worlds). Third generation, Internet ready phones mean that computers no longer reside only in the home, but are in the pockets of young people, challenging how parents and teachers monitor usage and impact. Cameras in mobile phones present opportunities for abuse unavailable with the early phones in the past, with far-reaching consequences. Photographs released into cyberspace cannot be fully retrieved and may turn up years later. Play Station® games now link to the Internet, enabling access direct from a so-called toy, and virtual worlds can be occupied readily from within a game, where avatars interact, controlled by individuals in the "real" world.

Not surprisingly, Smith et al. (2008) found that there were differences in the perceived impact of cyberbullying, according to the type experienced, with misuse of photographs and phone bullying being perceived as having the greatest impact, and chat room and e-mail incidents having the least impact. Chat room and e-mail incidents are more closely associated with the more static Web 1.0 environments, and one message from these findings is that the most impact is from the more sophisticated Web 2.0 environment which supports social networking and video sharing.

However, Palfrey (2008), writing that youth reports of (conventional) bullying remain more common than those of online harassment, reminds us that both forms coexist in young people's lives, making the possible impact for some, considerable. If bullying is considered to be a relationship problem (Pepler, Smith, & Rigby, 2004), then recognizing the impact that cyberbullying has on relationships is paramount. The "parallel universe" of cyberspace, which exists alongside family and schooling contexts, presents additional challenges for "real" world relationships. The conduct and maintenance of successful relationships in the "real" world is difficult enough for some (Mason, 2008), without the added dimension and complexity that cyberspace brings.

What is not evident from prevalence studies is the human dimension of this impact: the relationship cost of the experiences, emotions, and feelings associated with covert and cyberbullying. The current study aimed to address this by gathering narratives and stories from school communities about covert and cyberbullying, with a view to informing current understanding via authentic voice.

Method

Students, teachers, and school counselors confidentially self-recorded and self-edited their stories about covert and cyberbullying using Audacity®, a freely downloadable, digital recording software. Through analyzing these stories and narratives a greater depth of understanding of how this phenomenon is seen and understood, including its impact, was achieved.

There were four phases to this study, with Phases 1 through 3 operating in synchrony:

(1) digital recordings of stories/narratives about covert and cyberbullying were made;
(2) a dedicated project website from which the stories can be downloaded or listened to at anytime was constructed: http://www.deewr.gov.au/Schooling/NationalSafeSchools/Pages/research.aspx;
(3) narrative and thematic analyses of the stories;
(4) ongoing gathering of stories from the global community via the website. This will extend the database and capture the changing nature of cyberbullying as it evolves over time and across cultures.

Participants

Convenience and purposive sampling utilizing the maximum variation sampling (MVS) technique was employed. According to Patton (1987) this method provides information rich cases that enable "issues of central importance" (p. 52) to be determined. Also referred to as maximum heterogeneity sampling, MVS requires that participants are as different as possible from one another, so that when sample sizes are small (< 30) the diversity that is attained can approximate randomization.

Urban and semirural schools (single-sex boys', girls', and coeducational settings) (n = 10) from the government and nongovernment sectors in Adelaide, the capital city of South Australia, were purposively approached by the research team to ensure maximum diversity of settings. Principals were informed that the study concerned personal stories about covert and cyberbullying, and that one teacher and two students would be given training in pod casting techniques, so that they could return to school and gather further stories and train others in the use of the technology. Students who had firsthand knowledge or experiences from their social network and/or schooling community were selected to attend (n = 20) and appropriate consents were obtained. Teachers (n = 10) who volunteered came from English/Drama, Counseling, and Information & communication technology (ICT) domains, contributing to the diversity required. Students were from years 8 to 12 (aged 12–18 years) and equally represented by boys and girls. On separate occasions, school counselors (n = 6) attended similar recording sessions to tell stories from their school settings. Parent data are not reported in this paper. School counselors were invited via an electronic network of counselors and those who were available and chose to participate were from both metropolitan and country locations, working in both primary and secondary schools.

Procedure

Participants (teachers and students) were invited to attend a recording studio on one of two consecutive days. They self-selected into two groups, one per day, based on their availability. Counselors attended on a separate occasion. Led by the team of researchers each session undertook: an ice-breaker/Getting to Know You exercise; separate teacher and student small group discussions of what covert and cyberbullying meant to them, with responses recorded on Y Charts; and training in recording techniques, software, and pod casting, delivered by an ICT specialist. Following this, each participant wrote a brief outline of their story as a series of "dot points" in a word document on individual computers. Stories were then independently recorded by the participants and were self-edited using Audacity® software. This software is a free, downloadable recording package, which enables participants to see a visual representation of their voice and to edit it as required. Individuals were instructed to apply pseudonyms, to keep the stories brief (around 2–5 min), and to use the "dot points" as their guide, to avoid reading the narrative. All voices were subsequently altered so as to ensure anonymity when stories were included on a website. This was followed by the playing of the stories to the group, a general group discussion about each incident, and debrief.

Coding and Analysis: Narratives and "Y" Charts

Stories were transcribed and the researchers and members of an independent reference group comprised of educators and policy makers developed a process of intercoder agreement, for identifying key themes across all data sets (Miles & Huberman, 1994). This entailed independently reading the stories, noting ideas, concepts, and issues, and then determining a level of agreement across at least four researchers. Using *lean coding* (Creswell, 2008), only a few codes are assigned rather than many. Strauss (1987, cited in Neuman, 2006) refers to this as *open* coding, where the data are condensed into preliminary analytic categories or codes. In this model, *axial* coding forms the second review of the data, where the focus shifts to the initial coded themes, moving toward organizing ideas and identifying the key concepts. The final phase of analysis involves *selective* coding, seeking examples that illustrate themes and making comparisons and contrasts. Initial codes across all stories were subsequently reduced to capture the major ideas across the database, allowing broad themes to emerge.

Y Charts are a strategy used in schools by teachers to capture students' understandings and affective responses to new concepts or constructs. A page is divided into three areas, representing a large "Y," with sections labeled as "Looks Like," "Sounds Like," and "Feels Like." Students and teachers separately discussed their understanding of cyberbullying with reference to these headings: for example, Cyberbullying Looks Like ... recording their responses accordingly. These were then compared against the responses given for covert bullying. How these two forms of bullying "look," "sound," and "feel" to students, teachers and counselors in Australian schools adds voice to the definition debate.

Accuracy, Credibility, and Legitimacy of the Findings

Creswell (2008, p. 266) suggests that there are three primary forms of determining the accuracy and credibility of the findings in qualitative research: triangulation, member checking, and external audit.

Triangulation involves convergence with other sources of data. Denzin (1978) suggests four types of triangulation be employed which enable crosschecking across multiple sources. This study employed multiple: data sources/realities (stories/narratives from diverse participants), investigators (four authors), theoretical schemes for interpretation (thematic, narrative, and case study), and data gathering methods (stories and Y Charts).

Member checking involves the participants checking the accuracy of the researchers' interpretation. All stories were played to the group at the end of the session, and as part of the debrief and discussion, understandings and initial interpretations were clarified in the group setting.

Asking others outside the study to review different aspects of the research is known as an external audit. Several hundred students, teachers, and parents from at least 10 different schools across South Australia engaged with these stories during professional development sessions on understanding cyber relationships. Feedback from these groups provided us with confidence that we had interpreted the narratives accurately.

Research Findings and Discussion

The students in this study were purposively selected, having firsthand knowledge or experiences of covert and cyberbullying from their social networks and school communities, thus giving legitimate voice to these constructs. The teachers and counselors were easily able to recount stories that they had had direct contact within their school communities, indicating that cyber and covert bullying may not be isolated occurrences in schools and may involve more students than previously thought. Indeed, Smith et al. (2008, p. 378) reported that when focus groups reported on cyberbullying, they suggested that 67–100% would have experienced it, as distinct from surveys which reported 77% indicating "never" for involvement in cyberbullying.

Key themes reported here concern: definition and understanding; the interplay between overt and covert behaviors in cyberbullying; and the human dimension and impact of cyberbullying. Together these major themes reveal a complexity surrounding cyberbullying, which suggests that it is not simply conventional bullying transferred behind the screens via e-technologies.

Definitions, Understandings, and Impact of Covert and Cyberbullying

The "Y" Charts particularly reveal the impact and power elements of covert and cyberbullying. Both students and teachers reported covert and cyberbullying in schooling contexts to *look*, *sound* and to *feel* different from each other. Covert bullying behaviors looked like: *ostracism, exclusion,* and *manipulation and intimidation*, clearly reflecting behaviors associated with indirect, relational, and social forms of bullying and aggression (see Archer & Coyne, 2005; Owens, Shute, & Slee, 2000, 2004). Cyberbullying "looked" different, being variously reported as: *texting, e-mails shut down quickly, faceless, [like] hate pages, [like] hidden gangs, anonymous, instant, premeditated, and manipulated and altered images.* The behaviors which accompany these may well reflect the covert behaviors described above but what is immediately obvious is that the focus of what cyberbullying "looks like" at school involved *doing* something with technology to intimidate or put down another, perhaps repeatedly. Sending, typing, or filming are tangible acts and have a physical existence, such as a text, e-mail, or website.

Students and teachers discussed and recorded covert bullying in schooling contexts as "sounding like": *spreading rumors, fragmented whispering, and pay-outs and put-downs.* Again, these reflect behaviors associated with indirect, relational, and social forms of bullying and aggression. Cyberbullying, however, was described more according to the intensity and harm of the impact, rather than the behaviors, with it "sounding": *verbal, cruel, vicious, obscene, torturous, powerful* ... [like] *soft, urgent chatter around screens,* and even "sounded" *silent....* If the *behaviors* are similar to those described for covert bullying above, then when used in conjunction with technology, greater intensity is implied from these descriptors. Shariff and Strong-Wilson's definition (2005, cited in Shariff, 2008), defining peer-to-peer cyberbullying as comprising *covert, psychological* bullying conveyed through electronic media, resonates with these descriptors.

Participants responded that covert bullying in social network and schooling contexts is associated with feeling: *helpless, and powerless, ... and it feels hurtful ... and is bewildering, ... [it feels like] ... talking behind backs, and interrupted dialogues....* Describing how cyberbullying made them feel, however, captured the depth of the emotional impact and the powerlessness associated with bullying behind the screens. Cyberbullying felt: *unnerving, demeaning, inescapable, and unsafe,* making participants feel *vulnerable and alone...; like being trapped; ... [it felt like] a huge power imbalance* and [an] *invasion of privacy.* Patchin and Hinduja (2006) and Beran and Li (2007) reported that the negative effects of cyberbullying were not trivial, and the lived reality of the participants in this study offers clear support for this. Both the sense of powerlessness and helplessness necessary for the behaviors to be considered bullying and not simply acts of aggression between two parties of equal status are evident in these responses.

It is apparent that the participants conceived of covert bullying as the opposite of overt: occurring behind the *scenes* and employing indirect, relational, and social means to inflict psychological and emotional harm. Descriptors therefore offer support for the definition used in this study: that *covert bullying comprises typically repeated behaviours which are concealed, secret or clandestine, that inflict psychological/emotional harm through indirect/relational or social means where the target feels helpless and unable to retaliate.*

Cyberbullying was perceived similarly: to operate indirectly, relationally, and socially but from *behind the screens*: using texting, e-mails, hate pages, and altered images as tangible aspects of this form of bullying. With cyberbullying however, the descriptors indicate that the shift behind the screens has brought greater depth of impact. No explicit reference was made to repetition, rather it was implied by descriptors which were plural, indicating that the behaviors were not isolated or one-off: *e-mails, web pages, altered images, pay-outs and put-downs, and soft, urgent chatter around screens.*

Cyberbullying: Overt or Covert?

Participants in this study were invited to recount stories of *covert* bullying: Behaviors that occurred *behind the scenes.* Most, however, spontaneously reported incidents concerning the use of technology: where something may have been *covertly* filmed, sent, recorded, or typed, but was *then* used to bully the other person, rendering him/her powerless to do anything about it in the process. They therefore perceived cyberbullying to be a *form* of covert bullying. Palfrey (2008, p. 22) reported that cyberbullying may involve direct (such as chat or text messaging), semipublic (such as posting a harassing message on an e-mail list), or public communications (such as creating a website devoted to making fun of the victim). These examples reflect the relational and social forms of bullying, which can be direct as well as indirect (see Archer & Coyne, 2005).

On close examination, some narratives did not involve covert acts of bullying using technology, rather they were deliberately *overt*, as this example from the transcripts demonstrates: *[My] Friend broke up with her boyfriend ... so he abused her on MSN, then Piczo ... [he] sent her hate mail ... [he] stalked her across different sites and [her] phone.* Deliberately stalking or *overtly* abusing someone over social networking sites or e-mail, when the individual does *not* try to conceal their identity or remain hidden, are deliberate, aggressive acts *designed* to intimidate and to exercise power over another by their very presence in cyberspace. Sending hate mail, direct abuse, or visibly following or pursuing another across sites are clearly overt rather than covert acts. In the following summary from one of the narratives, an overt fight and the covert filming of it operate in concert with each other, demonstrating the complexity of this phenomenon, for example, *Two boys have an argument ... escalates into a physical fight ... filmed using mobile phone ... uploaded to the internet ... the loser [of the fight] was subsequently harassed and humiliated.... He isolated himself to avoid the taunts ... eventually leaving the school.*

It may be necessary to refer to *covert* cyberbullying or *overt* cyberbullying, in order to clarify and differentiate the behaviors involved. *Covert* cyberbullying reflects indirect, social, and relational behaviors resulting in exclusion, isolation, and the manipulation of friendships and relationships. These are evident when: rumors or images are spread from phone to phone without the targeted person knowing; anonymous derogatory websites are set up; or strangers intimidate from the security of anonymity.

Overt cyberbullying, such as deliberately taking intimate or other photographs, then using them to cause suffering to the victim, are explicit, deliberate acts that use technology to cause harm, for example, ... *The other girls kept opening the door while she was in there getting changed ... they got out a camera and every time they would open the door they would take a photo of this girl.*

Teachers' and counselors' narratives demonstrated how the complexity of relationship and friendship issues is being played out both behind the scenes *and* behind the screens, using both covert and overt acts of bullying with technology. For example, *Girls played "Spice Girls" and took erotic pictures of each other. Later, one girl cheats with her friend's boyfriend, to then discover that her "friend" has taken revenge and posted [on-line] the erotic pictures they had taken of her when playing, ... for all to see.* The covert act of uploading the photographs, combined with the overt act of making it public, demonstrates the interplay between these forms of cyberbullying. This interplay, however, is also known in conventional forms of relational and social bullying, where both direct and indirect behaviors interact, but the key difference is that the audience in the real world remains within a usually known social group. Cyberbullying involves a larger, mostly unknown, boundary-less audience, combined with anonymity for the perpetrator provided by the technology. Certainly, cyberbullying *employs* indirect, relational, and social means to inflict psychological harm and disrupt relationships, but it would seem that cyberbullying operates in a unique manner by enabling bullies to not only operate covertly and overtly but also to straddle the real and the cyber world somewhat simultaneously.

The narratives in this study have highlighted that the use of technology is enabling the transfer and continuation of bullying behaviors across boundaries, but the location of the start or end point is not necessarily clear, for example, [A] *boy was subtly bullied at school ... and then on MSN ... purely to get a reaction from him back at school....* In cycling between home and school, the method may be changed: what may be online at home possibly continues as physical or social bullying at school, only to change again back home to overt or covert bullying, for example, ... *boy claimed he was being picked on ... and then they used a mobile phone to rally others.* The line between the two environments, indeed between home or school and the wider world, is now blurred, as what has occurred within relationships at school can now be continued online by anyone. This has implications for schools as the cycle of abuse across jurisdictions, genders, and time will require clear processes and different strategies from school leadership and communities generally.

Cyberbullying as a Relationship Problem

Pepler et al. (2004) reported that bullying was a relationship problem, as it occurred in a social context. The disruption of relationships in the real world, as in the examples above, clearly leads to cyberbullying, and cyberbullying clearly impacts upon relationships. The cyclical nature of this is important, as it means that relationships may never be without interference in a technologically driven social world. As contemporary social contexts include social networking sites and video sharing sites, it seems evident that cyberbullying is indeed a relationship problem, cycling between two worlds, impacting in both. A brief examination of the content of the narratives reveals that they are predominantly concerned with interfering with relationships: for example, Boys used fights: *Sometimes fights are set up so a film can be taken and uploaded on to the internet* ... or stalking ... *It[stalking] was occurring through MSN, MySpace, Piczo* ... or *[There was] ganging up.* Dating relationships were put at risk and manipulated by others.... *She was dumped by his best friend just before the formal ... via text message.* Girls manipulated their friendships and peer relationships through blocking or password protected sites, giving only some access and excluding online.... *People posted comments about her ... [that she is a] slut ... [and] all the people she had had sex with....* One mother deliberately interfered with the dynamics of her daughter's peer relationships: *[Teacher] Year 7 girls had friendship issues.... Later discovered that she [daughter] had spoken with her mother ... and her mother had been on MSN chat ... sending messages back to the other girls, pretending to be her daughter....* Relationships are central to each narrative about covert or cyberbullying in this study.

Developmental differences (Smith, Madsen, & Moody, 1999) were also evident through the narratives. Younger students' stories focused upon manipulating friendships and peer relationships, with clear evidence of status-related incidents where there were social winners and losers. ... *A group of girls would send really nasty e-mails to those they didn't like....* Older students' stories shifted focus: To issues concerning sexuality and sexual experiences: girls stripped for webcam and mobile phones, or to please boyfriends or to join the so-called popular group; girls were filmed drunk at parties and others filmed them in vulnerable sexual situations *Girls were drunk ... [were] clandestinely filmed ... recorded inappropriate drunken and sexual behaviour....*

The range of relationship issues reported suggests that cyberbullying could be a normative component for contemporary relationships as individuals navigate and inhabit social networking and video sharing worlds. What used to occur in the privacy of one's own social network now is open to abuse by others, many of whom may be complete strangers. Certainly the range of examples and experiences related in this study was more diverse than expected from these participants, and the notion that cyberbullying is a relationship problem is supported.

The Human Dimension of Cyberbullying

From the transcripts of the student narratives, four key themes emerged concerning the impact and human dimension of covert and cyberbullying. These themes reflect the "issues of central importance" to which Patton (1987) referred. Cyberbullying in particular evoked: (1) strong negative feelings and emotions: for example, *anxiety, embarrassment, unhappiness, loneliness, sadness, powerlessness, depression, and increased aggression*, (2) fear: for example, of *going out, leaving home, going to school, invasion of privacy, and safety*, (3) an impact on self: for example, *loss of face, reputation damage, public humiliation, damage to self esteem, impact on schoolwork, and rejection*, and (4) disruption at different levels: for example, *I left the school, moved town, moved house, left boyfriend/girlfriend, and avoided others.* These authentic words and phrases powerfully illustrate the human dimension of cyberbullying: the depth of impact on individuals and families, ranging from psychological and emotional, to the physical impact of not attending school or changing schools, to moving towns and the break-up of relationships. The human dimension, as revealed through these narratives, is one of pain and suffering, of humiliation and anger, and of violation and vulnerability, and clearly supports previous studies which reported that the impact of cyberbullying is significant (Beran & Li, 2007; Patchin & Hinduja, 2006; Smith et al., 2008). Of note is that cyberbullying concerns the interruption to and breakdown of ordinary relationships, not just those of the bully or victim. For example, *I ... chose to leave the boyfriend ... had to leave the town to escape the humiliation....*

Summary

Although previous research indicates that traditional bullying is still more prevalent than cyberbullying (Palfrey, 2008; Smith et al., 2008), when stakeholders are asked directly about their experiences, many identify as having experienced it (Smith et al., 2008).

Qualitative research is employed to interpret reality, with a view to developing some theory that will explain that reality. This method emphasizes a detailed reading or examination of text to discover meaning embedded within it. Through constant comparison of the data with emerging themes and categories, theory can be postulated, from which hypotheses can eventually be generated and subsequently tested. It is therefore a more informal, interactive, subjective "voice" which employs an inductive process, where patterns and themes emerge from the data.

This study used a specific narrative methodology and has given "voice" to the experiences of students and school personnel regarding covert and cyberbullying, adding depth and breadth to the quantitative studies undertaken previously. In particular, cyberbullying was found to operate: both covertly and overtly via e-technologies; in concert with other bullying practices; and as a boundary-less, complex form of behavior which is perpetuated through a pattern of abuse that cycles between home and school. Participants indicated that there was a clear sense of helplessness associated with cyberbullying and that the power differential was clearly understood. The human dimension of covert and cyberbullying was given voice and found to involve more than anger and sadness. As previously described, cyberbullying evoked strong negative feelings and emotions; aroused fear and concerns for safety; and had a personal impact and disrupted and dislocated relationships. Furthermore, the lived realities of the participants in this study gave voice to understanding cyberbullying as a relationship problem.

Limitations and Future Research

Limitations to the study include the selection of the sample, which was small and purposive, and from only one city. The release of the website (www.cyberbullyingstories.org.au) will enable all visitors to contribute their stories, thus building a larger, broader sample, which should help to overcome this limitation. Self-selection bias is one limitation arising when participants are able to control if they participate (Palfrey, 2008), and while the teachers self-selected, they represented different roles within the profession across different schooling contexts and year levels in which they operated. Social expectation is another limitation, where participants seek to give responses they perceive are desired. In confidentially recording and editing their own stories, participants were able to recount their stories without receiving any nonverbal feedback such as approval or disapproval from the researchers.

In particular this study has highlighted the need for further debate regarding definitional issues and the personal experiences of those subject to this type of bullying. Beran and Li (2005) and Campbell (2005) suggested that cyberbullying was a new method for an old behavior. This may have seemed so initially, but as this study demonstrates, there is much that is complex about cyberbullying, and much that is different in an "always-on" society. The human dimension of covert and cyberbullying revolves around relationships that are struggling simultaneously in and across two domains: the real world and the cyber one. As technology continues to evolve toward Web 3.0 environments, researchers, educators, and policy makers will need to address the issue of bullying in a "boundary-less" world in order to fulfill the duty of care toward students in schools.

Acknowledgments

This project was funded by the Australian Government Department of Education, Employment and Workplace Relations (DEEWR) as one of two national studies into Covert Bullying. The project website will be available at www.cyberbullyingstories.org.au.

References

Archer, J., & Coyne, S. M. (2005). An integrated review of indirect, relational and social aggression. *Personality and Social Psychology Review, 9*, 212–230.

Beran, T., & Li, Q. (2005). Cyber-harassment: A study of a new method for an old behavior. *Journal of Educational Computing Research, 32*, 265–277.

Beran, T., & Li, Q. (2007). The relationship between cyberbullying and school bullying. *Journal of Student Wellbeing, 1*, 15–33.

Belsey, B. (2005). *Cyberbullying: An emerging threat to the always on generation.* Retrieved February 5, 2009, from http://www.cyberbullying.ca.

Belsey, B. (n.d.). *Cyberbullying.* Retrieved February 5, 2009, from http://www.cyberbullying.ca.

Campbell, M. A. (2005). Cyber bullying: An old problem in a new guise? *Australian Journal of Guidance and Counselling, 15*, 68–76.

Creswell, J. W. (2008). *Educational research: Planning, conducting and evaluating quantitative and qualitative research* (3rd ed.). NY: Pearson Merrill Prentice Hall.

Denzin, N. (1978). *Sociological methods: A sourcebook* (2nd ed.). NY: McGraw Hill.

Hinduja, S., & Patchin, J. W. (2008). Cyberbullying: An exploratory analysis of factors related to offending and victimization. *Deviant Behavior, 29*, 129–156.

Mason, K. (2008). Cyberbullying: A preliminary assessment for school personnel. *Psychology in the Schools, 45*, 323–348.

Miles, M. B., & Huberman, A. M. (1994). *Qualitative data analysis: An expanded sourcebook* (2nd ed.). CA: Sage.

Neuman, W. L. (2006). *Social research methods* (6th ed.). London: Allyn & Bacon.

Olweus, D. (1993). *Bullying at school: What we know and what we can do.* Oxford: Blackwell.

Ortega, R., Elipe, P., Mora-Merchán, J. A., Calmaestra, J., & Vega, E. (2009). *The emotional impact on victims of traditional bullying and cyberbullying: A study of Spanish adolescents. Zeitschrift für Psychologie / Journal of Psychology, 217*(4), 197–204.

Owens, L., Shute, R., & Slee, P. (2000). "Guess what I just heard!": Indirect aggression among teenage girls in Australia. *Aggressive Behavior, 26*, 67–83.

Owens, L., Shute, R., & Slee, P. T. (2004). Girls' aggressive behaviour. *The Prevention Researcher, 11*, 9–12.

Palfrey, J. (2008). *Enhancing child safety and on-line technologies.* Cambridge, MA: Final report of the Internet safety technical task force.

Patchin, J. W., & Hinduja, S. (2006). Bullies move beyond the schoolyard: A preliminary look at cyberbullying. *Youth Violence and Juvenile Justice, 4*, 148–169.

Patton, M. Q. (1987). *How to use qualitative methods in evaluation.* CA: Sage.

Pepler, D., Smith, P. K., & Rigby, K. (2004). Looking back and looking forward: Implications for making interventions work effectively. In P. K. Smith, D. Pepler, & K. Rigby (Eds.), *Bullying in schools, How successful can interventions be?* (pp. 307–325). Cambridge: Cambridge University Press.

Shariff, S. (2008). *Cyber-bullying: Issues and solutions for the school, the classroom and the home.* Abingdon: Routledge.

Smith, P. K., Madsen, K. C., & Moody, J. C. (1999). What causes the age decline in reports of being bullied at school? Towards a developmental analysis of the risks of being bullied. *Educational Researcher, 41*, 276–285.

Smith, P. K., Mahdavi, J., Carvalho, M., Fisher, S., Russell, S., & Tippett, N. (2008). Cyberbullying: Its nature and impact in secondary school pupils. *Journal of Child Psychology & Psychiatry, 49*, 376–385.

Willard, N. E. (2007a). *Cyber-safe kids, cyber-savvy teens: Helping young people learn to use the Internet safely and responsibly.* San Francisco: Jossey-Bass.

Willard, N. E. (2007b). The authority and responsibility of school officials in responding to cyberbullying. *Journal of Adolescent Health, 41*, S64–S65.

Wolak, J., Mitchell, K., & Finkelhor, D. (2007). Does online harassment constitute bullying? An exploration of online harassment by known peers and online-only contacts. *Journal of Adolescent Health, 41*, S51–S58.

Barbara Spears

School of Education
University of South Australia
Magill Campus
Magill
South Australia 5072
Australia
Tel. +61 8 830 24500
Fax +61 8 830 24394
E-mail Barbara.Spears@unisa.edu.au

The Emotional Impact on Victims of Traditional Bullying and Cyberbullying

A Study of Spanish Adolescents

Rosario Ortega,[1] Paz Elipe,[2] Joaquín A. Mora-Merchán,[3] Juan Calmaestra,[1] and Esther Vega[1]

[1]Department of Psychology, University of Córdoba, Spain
[2]Department of Psychology, University of Jaén, Spain
[3]Department of Developmental and Educational Psychology, University of Seville, Spain

Abstract. We examine the emotional impact caused to victims of bullying in its traditional form, both directly and indirectly, as well as bullying inflicted by use of new technologies such as mobile phones and the Internet. A sample of 1,671 adolescents and young people responded to a questionnaire which asked if they had been victims of various forms of bullying, as well as the emotions this caused. The results show that although traditional bullying affected significantly more young people than cyberbullying, the latter affected one in ten adolescents. Analysis of the emotions caused showed that traditional bullying produced a wide variety of impacts, with the victims being divided into five different emotional categories, while indirect bullying and cyberbullying presented a narrower variety of results with the victims being classifiable into just two groups: Those who said that they had not been emotionally affected and those who simultaneously suffered from a wide variety of negative emotions. The influence of age, gender, and severity on each emotional category is also analyzed.

Keywords: bullying, cyberbullying, emotions, victimization, adolescents

There is broad agreement that bullying can be defined as a form of aggression that occurs when an individual or group intimidates, excludes, harasses, or mistreats, another or others, directly (physically or verbally) or indirectly (threats, insults, isolation, destruction, or theft of belongings, etc.) (Olweus, 1999). A complex power imbalance arises among those involved, making it difficult for victims to defend themselves. Episodes are intentionally repeated over time until they constitute a relational problem and also one for the coexistence of those involved (Ortega & Mora-Merchán, 2000, 2008). When victims manage to defend themselves promptly, pathological relationships and dependence on the aggressor are diminished and negative effects may be minor. This, in fact, is what many victims do. However, when extended over a period of months, and if the victim finds no help or support, then the phenomenon can become particularly negative and the effects on the mental health of victims extremely pernicious (Aluede, Adeleke, Omoike, & Afen-Akpaida, 2008; Dyer & Teggart, 2007).

Victims of bullying always are affected by any vulnerability, but this could be mediated by diverse conditions and factors (Hunter & Borg, 2006; Kochenderfer-Ladd, 2004; Kochenderfer-Ladd & Ladd, 2001). Frequently, internalized fear may accompany the feeling of being defenseless, while an angry and reactive fear may feed a stress reaction. Stress, itself associated with reactive emotions such as anger, may support an attitude of either confrontation or avoidance and flight (Lazarus, 2000). Some victims show an adaptive resilience which allows them to soften the emotional impact of aggression. It is possible that this gives them the emotional strength to allow them to manage this adverse situation successfully (Christle, Jolivette, & Nelson, 2000; Schwartz, Proctor, & Chien, 2001). Others, however, experience negative feelings over which they have little control and which affect their well-being and influence the environment in which they develop and relate to others (Graham & Juvonen, 2001).

Over recent years the phenomenon of bullying has become more complex in view of the widespread use of Information and Communication Technologies (ICT) by adolescents and young people. This has opened a new line of research on cyberbullying. In Spain, a nationwide study by the Defensor Del Pueblo-UNICEF (2006), which included questions about victimization and aggression using

DOI: 10.1027/0044-3409.217.4.197

ICT, found that 5.5% of students reported having been cyber-victims, whereas 4.8% admitted they were cyber-aggressors. Our preliminary studies (Calmaestra, Ortega, & Mora-Merchán, 2008; Mora-Merchán & Ortega, 2007; Ortega, Calmaestra, & Mora-Merchán, 2008) performed with specific instruments for the study of cyberbullying have shown that including occasionally as well as severely, approximately 20% of secondary and high school students are involved in this phenomenon.

Cyberbullying is structured by a relational dynamic with at least two well-defined roles: aggressor and victim. However, its communication channel, instantaneity, and the lack of face-to-face contact bring differential characteristics: (a) the communication scenario of the actors involved, which apart from not being direct, could be extended in time and space; (b) the possible anonymity of the aggressor (some studies have found that in 20–30% of occasions the victims are unaware of their cyber-aggressor's identity, although in 50–60% of cases the phenomenon occurs among students from the same educational center: Slonje & Smith, 2008; Smith et al., 2008); and (c) its indirect character, as in the case of cyberbullying, the aggressive behavior is always mediated by the technological resource the aggressor uses and through which the victims receive the aggression (Ortega, Elipe, & Calmaestra, in press).

In this paper we hypothesize that despite its specificities, cyberbullying retains the same basic roles (victim and aggressor) and different levels of severity (occasional and severe) as found in traditional bullying. However, we hypothesize that the emotional effects on the victim are different. Specifically, we analyzed the similarities and differences of this impact according to the specific type of bullying suffered (traditional bullying: direct and indirect and cyberbullying: via mobile phone and the Internet) in relation to age (school-year of the participant) and severity of the aggression (occasional and more frequent). The specific objectives were:

(1) To describe the prevalence of different kinds of victimization in the sample: direct and indirect bullying, cyberbullying (via mobile phone and the Internet) in relation to two levels of severity (occasional and more frequent), age and gender.
(2) To analyze the emotional impact reported by victims of both types of bullying (traditional and cyberbullying) and establish differential emotional profiles in both types of suffering and in relation to severity of bullying, age, and gender.

Method

Participants

The original study sample was composed of 1,755 students from seven secondary schools in Córdoba, Spain randomly selected from the provincial school network. The data of 4.9% of participants whose responses were inconsistent or who had not completed important parts of the questionnaire were excluded. As a result, the final sample was formed of 1,671 adolescents (51.3% males and 48.7% females) distributed in three educational levels/ages: 1st year of Compulsory Secondary Education, $n = 539$ (12–13 year olds; 55.8% males and 44.2% females), 3rd year of Compulsory Secondary Education, $n = 534$ (14–15 year olds; 50.1% males and 49.9% females), and 1st year of High School (Bachillerato), $n = 598$ (16–17 year olds; 48.5% males and 51.5% females).

Instrument

We used the *DAPHNE Questionnaire* (Genta et al., 2009), developed within the framework of the project "An investigation into forms of peer-peer bullying at school in preadolescent and adolescent groups: New instruments and preventing strategies". A translation into Spanish of this questionnaire was used for this study. It is made up of three self-report sections: "About you" (35 items), "About your school" (11 items), and "About bullying and cyberbullying" (37 items). The "About bullying and cyberbullying" section collects information, through multiple-choice questions, about five areas: students' access to ICT (3 items), direct bullying (5 items), indirect bullying (5 items), cyberbullying via mobile phone (12 items), and via the Internet (12 questions). With the objective of improving the validity of responses, following the recommendations of Solberg & Olweus, 2003, the following definitions of bullying and cyberbullying were provided in the questionnarie: "Bullying is behavior carried out by an individual, or a group, which is repeated over time in order to hurt, threaten or frighten another individual with the intention to cause distress. It is different from other aggressive behavior because it involves an imbalance of power which leaves the victim defenseless"; "Cyberbullying is a new form of bullying which involves the use of mobile phones (texts, calls, video clips) or the Internet (e-mail, instant messaging, chat rooms, and websites) or other forms of ICT to deliberately harass, threaten, or intimidate someone".

Next, examples of direct bullying were provided (hitting, insulting, making fun of someone, etc.) and questions were asked about this type of bullying: (a) frequency of victimization, (b) feelings associated with victimization, (c) frequency of aggression, (d) frequency of observing episodes of this type, and (e) behavior when observing episodes of this type. The same sequence of questions was used to evaluate indirect bullying (lying or spreading false rumors about someone behind their back, etc.). In order to examine cyberbullying, two types of cyberbullying were distinguished; aggression using mobile phone (upsetting phone calls, taking photographs and/or videos, e.g., being flamed, happy slapping, . . ., abusive text messages) and aggression via the Internet (malicious or threatening e-mails directly to the victim, or about the victim to others, intimidation or abuse in chat rooms, abusive instant messages, websites where secrets or personal details are revealed in an abusive way or where nasty or unpleasant comments are being made, social networking websites, file sharing websites, and blogs). These were examined using a parallel structure used to explore traditional bullying, but with the addition of further detailed items not reported in this paper.

Procedure

Once the educational centers which took part in the study were selected, we made a first approach to request collaboration and consent for participation in the study. Students enrolled in all the school-years selected for the research were then contacted and asked to participate. After obtaining the appropriate consent, the questionnaire was handed out during class sessions. A member of the research team was in charge of handing out the questionnaires and gave precise instructions. Anonymity and voluntary participation were emphasized as well as the importance of honest answers. The concepts of bullying and cyberbullying were explained and any doubts expressed by the students as they answered the questionnaire were cleared up. The average time needed to complete the questionnaire was about 45 min.

Data Analysis

Identification of the victims was established from the answers to the questions: "Have you been bullied . . . over the last two months?" for each type (direct, indirect, via the Internet, and via mobile phone). The response options for all cases were "I haven't been bullied", "Once or twice", "Two or three times a month", "Once a week", and "Several times a week". When the victim reported having suffered this kind of aggression "Once or twice" it was considered to be occasional aggression. When the victim reported having suffered aggression more frequently, this was considered to be severe aggression.

As we analyzed the categorical variables, chi-square contrasts and, when pertinent, contrasts ratios (*z* test) were used. Bonferroni correction was used to determine the level of significance of the *z* test because we made multiple comparisons.

In order to obtain groups of emotions, a hierarchical cluster analysis was used. The amalgamation (linkage) rule used was Ward's method and the measure distance was the percentage of disagreement. A two-phase cluster analysis was used in order to obtain groups of individuals based on emotional impact. This method is an algorithm in two steps: (1) bringing together previous clustering of the cases into many small sub-clusters and (2) clustering the resulting sub-clusters of the previous clustering. In the first step Schwarz's Bayesian Information Criterion is calculated for each number of clusters within a specified range and the result is used to find the initial estimation of the number of clusters. In a second step, the initial estimation is refined to find the highest relative increase in the distance between the two nearest clusters in each step of hierarchical grouping. The distance measurement used was log-likelihood. The distance between two clusters is related to the decrease in log-likelihood as they are combined into one cluster.

The level of significance adopted for all the analyses was $p < .05$.

Results

Prevalence of Traditional Bullying and Cyberbullying Victims

Table 1 shows the prevalence of traditional bullying (direct and indirect) against cyberbullying (via mobile phone and the Internet) although the number of students severely affected is not very high in our study. Overall, we found that 25% of participants were affected by some kind of bullying. Some victims had suffered exclusively traditional bullying (direct, indirect, or both; 15%), others exclusively cyberbullying (via mobile phone, the Internet, or both; 5%), and some both types of bullying (multivictimization; 5%).

Age (school grade) was examined in relation to all four types of bullying (indirect and direct bullying, cyberbullying via mobile phone and via the Internet). There were no significant differences for indirect bullying or for cyberbullying via the Internet. For direct bullying, victim rates were higher in the 1st and 3rd years of Secondary Education (14.8% and 12.4%, respectively) than in High School (5.4%), $\chi^2(2, 1{,}660) = 28.82$, $p < .01$. For cyberbullying by mobile phone, victim rates were higher in 3rd year students in Secondary Education (5.9%) than among those in 1st year (2.3%) or in High School (4.6%), $\chi^2(2, 1{,}641) = 8.70$, $p = .01$.

Gender was similarly examined in relation to all four types of bullying. There were no significant differences for indirect bullying. For direct bullying, victims rates were higher for males (13.0%) than females (8.3%), $\chi^2(1, 1{,}661) = 9.67$, $p < .01$. In contrast, more females reported being victims of cyberbullying both via mobile phone (6.3% females vs. 2.4% males), $\chi^2(1, 1{,}642) = 15.09$, $p < .01$, and via the Internet (9.1% females vs. 6% males), $\chi^2(1, 1{,}649) = 5.69$, $p = .02$.

Emotional Impact of Traditional Bullying and of Cyberbullying

The emotional impact the bullying generated in the victims was assessed through questions: "How did you feel when

Table 1. Percentage of victims by type and severity of aggression

	Direct bullying	Indirect bullying	Mobile cyberbullying	Internet cyberbullying
Haven't been bullied	89.3	84.2	95.7	92.5
Occasional victimization	7.5	12.4	3.7	6.2
Severe victimization	3.2	3.4	0.5	1.3

Table 2. Emotions reported by victims of traditional bullying and cyberbullying

	Not bothered	Embarrassed	Angry	Upset	Stressed	Worried	Afraid	Alone	Defenseless	Depressed	Other
Direct bullying	23.4	*25.7*	*41.5*	17.5	10.5	15.8	15.2	13.5	11.7	17.0	12.3
Indirect bullying	*26.2*	11.7	*40.6*	23.4	9.0	19.1	5.5	7.4	5.1	14.8	9.0
Mobile cyberbullying	*35.8*	6.0	*31.3*	22.4	7.5	23.9	13.4	7.5	13.4	13.4	10.4
Internet cyberbullying	*43.9*	6.5	*29.3*	17.1	8.9	15.4	8.9	7.3	5.7	10.6	11.4

Note. The two categories more selected are shown italicized and the two least selected are shown in gray shade for each type of bullying.

bullied ... over the last two months?" This question was formulated for each type of bullying: direct, indirect, via mobile phone, and via the Internet. In all cases the participant could choose one or several of the following options: "I haven't been bullied over the last two months", "Embarrassed", "Worried", "Upset", "Afraid and scared", "Alone and isolated", "Defenseless, no one can do anything for me", "Depressed", "Stressed, tense", "Not bothered", "Angry", and "Other (please state)".

Table 2 shows the emotions reported, by victims of the four types of bullying. We analyzed these in relation to age (school grade), gender, and to severity of bullying (occasional or frequent). No significant associations were found for age.

Regarding gender, generally a higher number of females stated that they felt diverse negative emotions. For direct bullying, more females than males stated that they felt afraid (25.4% vs. 9.3%), $\chi^2(1, 171) = 8.04$, $p = .01$. For indirect bullying more females than males stated that they felt worried (26.1% vs. 11%), $\chi^2(1, 256) = 9.33$, $p < .01$, depressed (21.0% vs. 7.6%), $\chi^2(1, 256) = 9.02$, $p < .01$, and angry (47.1% vs. 33.1%), $\chi^2(1, 256) = 5.21$, $p = .02$; more males than females stated that they were not bothered (32.2% vs. 21.0%), $\chi^2(1, 256) = 4.12$, $p = .04$. For cyberbullying via mobile phone, more females than males stated that they felt worried (30.6% vs. 5.6%), $\chi^2(1, 67) = 4.55$, $p = .03$; more males than females said that they were not bothered (55.6% vs. 28.6%), $\chi^2(1, 67) = 4.17$, $p = .04$. Via the Internet, more females than males stated that they felt stressed (13.7% vs. 2.0%), $\chi^2(1, 123) = 4.99$, $p = .03$, and angry (37.0% vs. 18.0%), $\chi^2(1, 123) = 5.17$, $p = .02$.

Regarding severity of the bullying (occasional or more frequent), generally severe victims reported more negative emotions. For direct bullying, more severe than occasional victims stated that they were embarrassed (35.8% vs. 21.2%), $\chi^2(1, 171) = 4.12$, $p = .04$, upset (26.4% vs. 13.6%), $\chi^2(1, 171) = 4.18$, $p = .04$, and depressed (32.1% vs. 10.2%), $\chi^2(1, 171) = 12.46$, $p < .01$; while more occasional than severe victims reported that they were not bothered (29.7% vs. 9.4%), $\chi^2(1, 171) = 8.35$, $p < .01$. For indirect bullying, more severe than occasional victims stated that they were depressed (28.6% vs. 11%), $\chi^2(1, 256) = 10.69$, $p < .01$. For cyberbullying via mobile phone, more severe than occasional victims stated that they felt alone (33.3 vs. 3.4%), $\chi^2(1, 67) = 10.08$, $p < .01$, and stressed (33.3% vs. 3.4%), $\chi^2(1, 67) = 10.08$, $p < .01$. For cyberbullying via the Internet more severe than occasional victims stated that they felt stress (25.0% vs. 5.8%), $\chi^2(1, 123) = 7.56$, $p = .01$.

Clustering of Emotions in Traditional Bullying and Cyberbullying

With the objective of identifying the emotions that were most related to each other, a cluster analysis was carried out with the emotions (excluding the "Other" category). Distance matrices were calculated for each type of bullying (these can be obtained from the first author). The analysis of the dendrograms obtained showed different groupings of emotions for the four different types of bullying, as shown in Table 3.

The most differentiated grouping of emotions appeared in direct traditional bullying in which six groups were identified. In indirect bullying and cyberbullying by mobile phone, a similar grouping appeared, but with only five groups of emotions. In cyberbullying via the Internet, a less differentiated group, with three groups was found. In each

Table 3. Summary of emotion groups from the cluster analysis for each type of bullying

Direct bullying	Indirect bullying	Mobile phone cyberbullying	Internet cyberbullying
Alone	Alone	Alone	Alone
Defenseless	Defenseless	Defenseless	Defenseless
Depressed	Depressed Stressed Afraid Embarrassed	Depressed Stressed Afraid Embarrassed	Depressed Stressed Afraid Embarrassed Worried Upset
Embarrassed			
Worried Afraid	Worried	Worried	
Upset Stressed	Upset	Upset	
Angry	Angry	Angry	Angry
Not bothered	Not bothered	Not bothered	Not bothered

case, the emotions "not bothered" and "angry" we found to be independent from the rest.

Emotional Profiles of Victims of Traditional Bullying and Cyberbullying

A separate cluster analysis for each type of bullying (direct, indirect, cyberbullying via mobile phone, and the Internet) was carried out in order to establish the emotional profile of the victims. The variables included were the victims' answers to questions relating to the emotions they had felt after suffering the bullying, excluding the "Other" category. All the victims were included regardless of the severity of the aggression. The resulting victim profiles are shown in Figures 1–4. In the case of direct bullying, five distinctive clusters appeared, whereas both in traditional indirect bullying and cyberbullying (via mobile phone and the Internet) just two clusters were identified. The nature of the clusters is commented on below, together with their composition in relation to age (grade level), gender, and severity of victimization.

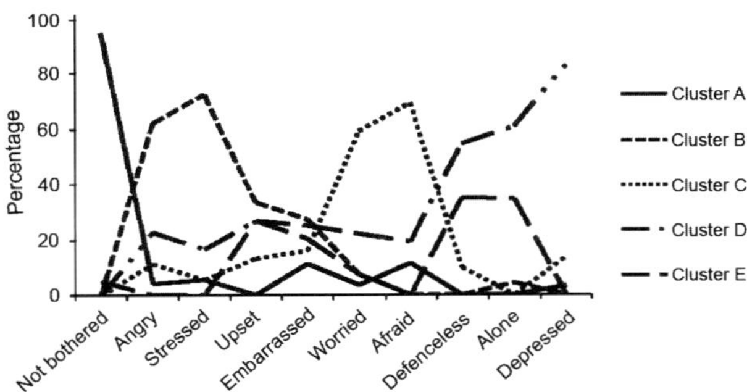

Figure 1. Victims who reported feeling each emotion distributed by cluster: Direct bullying.

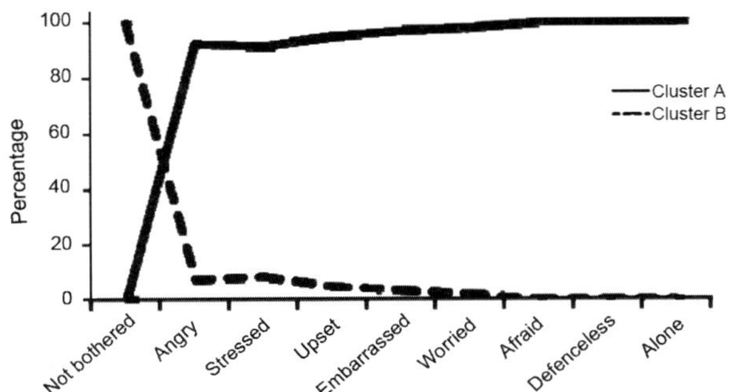

Figure 2. Victims who reported feeling each emotion distributed by cluster: Indirect bullying.

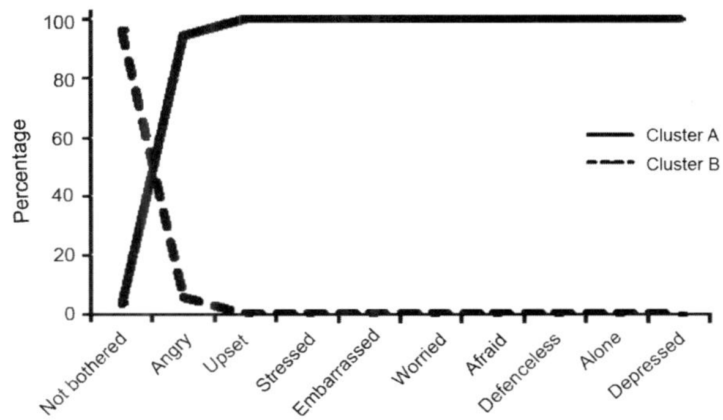

Figure 3. Victims who reported feeling each emotion distributed by cluster: Cyberbullying via the Internet.

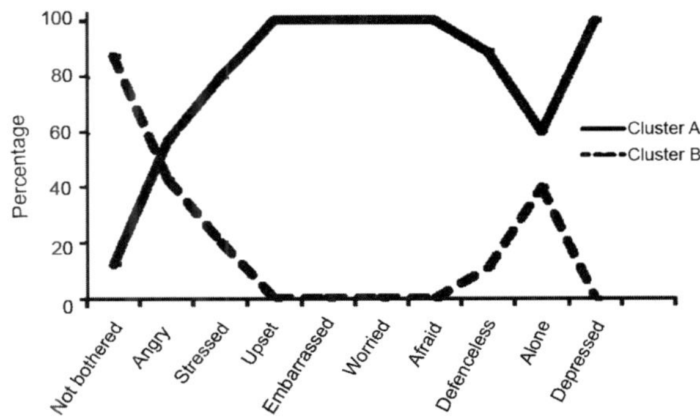

Figure 4. Victims who reported feeling each emotion distributed by cluster: Cyberbullying via mobile phone.

Direct Bullying

Figure 1 shows different "emotional profiles" for five groups of victims. The A cluster is marked by a high proportion of "not bothered" and a low proportion of the rest of the emotions. The B cluster is marked by a high proportion of "stressed" and "angry", whereas "depressed", "not bothered", and "afraid" are not mentioned by any of the victims. The C cluster has a high proportion of "worried" and "afraid", whereas "not bothered" is not mentioned. The D cluster covers "depressed", "alone", and "defenseless", whereas "not bothered" is absent. The E cluster is marked by the absence of "angry" victims and by a moderate presence of other emotions: upset, embarrassment, defenselessness, and loneliness.

No significant differences appeared in cluster composition in terms of age. For gender, there was a higher proportion of females than males in the "worried and afraid" cluster (25.4% vs. 9.3%), but this was not significant on chi-square analysis; differences in proportions in the rest of the clusters were less substantial.

The severity of the bullying was markedly associated with the composition of the cluster, $\chi^2(4, 171) = 14.95$, $p = .01$. The proportion of occasional victims in the "not bothered" cluster was significantly higher than severe victims (28.0% vs. 9.4%). On the other hand, in the "alone, defenseless, and depressed" cluster there was a higher proportion of severe than occasional victims (28.3% vs. 10.2%).

Indirect Bullying

Two clusters emerged in relation to the emotions that the victims of indirect bullying recorded; see Figure 2. Cluster A covered all the (negative) emotions, with an absence of "not bothered". Conversely cluster B victims were "not bothered" and were low or absent on the other emotions.

No significant differences were found in the clusters in relation to age or the severity of the bullying. However, there were gender differences, $\chi^2(1, 256) = 4.12$, $p = .04$ with a higher proportion of females than males in cluster A (79.0% vs. 67.8%) and a corresponding higher proportion of males in cluster B.

Cyberbullying via the Internet

The clusters produced for victims via the Internet showed two groups with a very similar configuration to those obtained for indirect bullying, see Figure 3.

There were no significant differences in the clusters, in terms of age or the severity of the bullying. There were gender differences, $\chi^2(1, 123) = 4.75$, $p = .03$, with a higher proportion of females than males in cluster A (65.8% vs. 46.0%) and a corresponding higher proportion of males in cluster B.

Cyberbullying via Mobile Phone

There were two clusters of victims of cyberbullying via mobile phone, as for those obtained for indirect bullying and bullying via the Internet, but with some differences with respect to those profiles, especially as regards the "alone" emotion, see Figure 4.

There were no significant differences in the clusters, in terms of age or the severity of the bullying. There were gender differences, $\chi^2(1, 67) = 7.20$, $p < .01$, with a higher proportion of females than males in cluster A (59.2% vs. 22.2%) and a corresponding higher proportion of males in cluster B.

Discussion

Our results indicated, as expected, that direct and indirect forms of bullying which do not involve technology are more common than those which use ICT. While nearly two in ten felt themselves to be a victim of some traditional form of bullying, only one in ten had a similar experience via technological means such as a mobile phone or the Internet. It is worth noting that one in five victims perceives themselves as victims of both types of bullying. These data are in line with general trends described by other studies (Olweus, 1999; Ortega & Mora-Merchán, 2000, 2008; Smith et al., 2004). However, it is clear that cyberbullying might gradually substitute more traditional forms (Smith et al., 2008).

Again as expected, being a victim decreased significantly from 12 to 17 years. However, in the case of cyberbullying there was a significant peak in victimization by mobile phone around the age of 14. This differs from trends found in traditional bullying. There is more than one possible explanation for this, but it could be related to the fact that it is during the years of midadolescence (14–15 years) that dating and courtship begin (Menesini & Nocentini, 2008; Ortega, Ortega-Rivera, & Sánchez, 2008; Ortega, Sánchez, Ortega-Rivera, & Viejo, 2008). Contemporary dating and courtship seem to include the widespread use of ICT, and mobile phones in particular, but also the Internet. This argument is reinforced by the fact that it is females who report experiencing more cyberbullying as victims. Gender differences are also an important factor in traditional direct bullying where most victims are males. The classical gender differences in the case of indirect bullying were not observed in this study, which might indicate a gender "evenness" trend in this phenomenon. This gender "evenness" may be more apparent in cases of psychological and relational bullying than in physical and verbal aggression (which were more likely to involve males).

The main objective of this study was the analysis of the emotional impact caused by victimization, and the search for emotional profiles that might indicate the specific suffering that each of these forms of bullying causes for the victim. According to Fernández-Abascal (2003) it is possible to distinguish among families of primary emotions. Following this idea, we would propose classifying victims' emotions into five different groups: "not bothered", referring to an absence of a specific emotion; those related to a basic emotion of fear – worried, afraid; those related to anger, with distinct levels of intensity – angry, stressed, and upset; those associated with sadness – depressed, defenseless, alone; and one moral emotion – shame. Our results showed that the most common emotional response is being angry, especially in direct bullying, together with a range of other negative emotions; but also that an important number of victims feel emotionally strong enough to state that these attacks had not bothered them, particularly in relation to cyberbullying.

This last finding can be interpreted in different ways. Maybe the difference is associated with the perceived emotional distance from the aggression and/or aggressor when a technological resource is mediating the aggression, or when the aggressor is unknown, both of which are defining features of cyberbullying (Slonje & Smith, 2008; Smith et al., 2008). However, the significant proportion of participants who were "not bothered" in response to all kinds of bullying could be interpreted in terms of personal capacity to not feel affected (Christle et al., 2000). Also in direct bullying, embarrassment stands out; an emotion which is hardly ever mentioned in the case of cyberbullying. The perception of anonymity could be interpreted as an element which protects victims from that disturbing social emotion as many cyberbullying attacks are not obvious to others and remain "private" between the aggressor and victim.

Age was not a significant variable in terms of the emotional responses, a fact that requires interpretation. It seems reasonable to suggest that there is a stability of emotional literacy during the adolescent years studied here.

With regard to gender, it was generally the females, more than the males, who stated that they felt a number of negative emotions at the same time in the face of the different types of attack. These results could be related to the finding that females show a higher level of precision in the perception and understanding of emotions (Barrett, Lane, Sechrest, & Schwartz, 2000; Mestre, Guil, Lopes, Salovey, & Gil-Olarte, 2006) as well as the finding that girls place more importance on social contacts and friendships through ICT (Thelwall, 2008). It is also possible that males do not feel inclined to admit that victimization affects them emotionally. We are not dealing here with ordinary conflicts or fights, but rather an abuse of power and unequal responsibilities, all of which could have more impact and in more diverse ways on females.

Severity of victimization was associated with some differing emotional consequences. A higher proportion of severe victims, regardless of type of bullying, reported feelings such as embarrassment, stress, upset, depression, and loneliness. These results support the idea that exposure to prolonged episodes of bullying, of whatever type, worsens the emotional impact on the victims (Aluede et al., 2008).

In conclusion, this study aimed at describing the emotional profiles associated with both traditional bullying and cyberbullying. Our results produced a higher degree of discrimination of emotions linked to victimization in the case of traditional direct bullying, where five victim profiles can be differentiated, whereas only two victim profiles are found in indirect bullying. These emotional profiles can be assumed into the theoretical classification presented above. The differences between traditional direct bullying and the other forms, in terms of diversity in the emotional response, could be interpreted as a result of heterogeneity of behaviors included in direct bullying (verbal and physical attacks, threatening, and taking belongings). These differences also could be a result of the face-to-face characteristic of these interactions, where victims have more emotional information about their aggressors. Consequently, victims are perhaps better able to "read" the intentions of the aggressor and this may affect their emotional response to the aggression. However, it is necessary that further research is conducted to explore these hypotheses.

In general cyberbullying produces emotional profiles similar to indirect bullying, with some smaller differences related to whether the bullying is via mobile phone or the Internet. Bullying via mobile phone is less likely to provoke feelings of loneliness than bullying via the Internet or indirect bullying. This is interesting and further research is necessary to understand the differences found here.

These data do not support the hypothesis we set out when we predicted that there would be a different impact of cyberbullying compared to traditional bullying. On the contrary, the data reinforce the characterization of cyberbullying as an indirect form of bullying (Slonje & Smith, 2008). However, "not bothered" and "angry" are two independent emotions in all types of bullying. Taken together, these results reinforce the suggestion that it is important to consider the four types of bullying studied as different, but related, phenomena. It is worth noting that anger appears as an independent emotion in all types of bullying. This emotion seems to be a key element in the emotional dysregulation that some victims show (Garner & Lemerise, 2007; Kelly, Schwartz, Gorman, & Nakamoto, 2008; Schwartz et al., 2001). It would be interesting to examine the role of anger in the different emotional profiles more precisely, taking into account the diverse roles involved in bullying.

The emotional profiles do not show differences in relation to the age groups studied. There are consistent gender differences, with those "not bothered" comprising more male victims and those emotionally affected more often female.

Severity did turn out to be a decisive factor in the analysis of the emotional profiles but only for direct bullying. The "not bothered" profile corresponded significantly to the occasional bullying phenomenon whereas the "alone, defenseless and depressed" profile corresponded to severe victimization, which confirms the negative effect that the persistent suffering of this kind of experience can cause (Dyert & Teggart, 2007). It is possible that some of the factors which differentiate cyberbullying and indirect bullying from direct bullying (e.g., the absence of face-to-face contact) may mediate the relationship between the frequency of the aggression and its emotional impact. However, it is not possible to examine this hypothesis using the data from this study.

This study has a number of limitations which will have to be addressed in future research. It is evident that a local sample may contain cultural biases which may not be present in international studies. Moreover, the reliance on a self-report instrument means that we have to be cautious in making any generalizations in relation to the emotional consequences of bullying in its different forms. However, even though this has been an exploratory study, our results point to an interesting research line that could, if these trends are confirmed in other studies, establish a framework of the emotional effects caused by indirect bullying (traditional and cyberbullying) in contrast to direct bullying. Future research needs to identify the specific factors responsible for the different emotional impact of aggression on the victims and which of these could be useful to manage and minimize such impact. In this respect, the analysis of the ways in which individuals process social and emotional information, as well as emotion regulation, could be particularly interesting.

Acknowledgments

This study was carried out in the framework of National Research Plan (SEJ-2007-60673) and HUM-02175 Excellence Research Projects of Andalusian PAIDI, and the European Daphne Project (JLS/2096/DAP-l/241YC 30-CE-0120045/00-79). The first author received support from the Prof-Ex. Programme (2008-0106) by the Spanish MICINN to be a Visiting Professor at the University of Greenwich, UK. The authors are grateful for the support received.

References

Aluede, O., Adeleke, F., Omoike, D., & Afen-Akpaida, J. (2008). A review of the extent, nature, characteristics and effects of bullying behaviour in school. *Journal of Instructional Psychology, 35*, 151–158.

Barrett, L. F., Lane, R., Sechrest, L., & Schwartz, G. (2000). Sex differences in emotional awareness. *Personality and Social Psychology Bulletin, 26*, 1027–1035.

Calmaestra, J., Ortega, R., & Mora-Merchán, J. A. (2008). Las TIC y la convivencia Un estudio sobre formas de acoso en el ciberespacio. *Investigación en la Escuela, 64*, 93–103.

Christle, C. A., Jolivette, K., & Nelson, C. M. (2000). Youth aggression and violence: risk, resilience, and prevention. *Council for Exceptional Children* (ERIC EC Digest #E602. Retrieved September 20, 2008, from http://www.cec.sped.org/AMT/Template.cfm?Section=Home&CONTENTID=3560&TEMPLATE=/CM/ContentDisplay.cfm).

Defensor Del Pueblo-UNICEF. (2006). *Violencia escolar: el maltrato entre iguales en la educación secundaria obligatoria. 1999–2006*. Madrid: Publicaciones de la Oficina del Defensor del Pueblo.

Dyer, K., & Teggart, T. (2007). Bullying experiences of child and adolescent mental health service-users: A pilot survey. *Child Care in Practice, 13*, 351–365.

Fernández-Abascal E. G. (2003). Procesamiento emocional. In G. Fernández-Abascal, F., P. Jiménez Sánchez, & M. D. Martín Díaz (Eds.), *Emoción y motivación: La adaptación humana* (Vol. 1, pp. 47–93). Madrid: Centro de Estudios Ramón Areces.

Garner, P. W., & Lemerise, E. A. (2007). The roles of behavioral adjustment and conceptions of peer and emotions in preschool children's peer victimization. *Development and Psychopathology, 19*, 57–71.

Genta, M. L., Brighi, A., Guarini, A., Ortega, R., Mora-Merchán, J. A., Calmaestra, J., et al. (2009). *Prevalence and forms of cyberbullying and traditional bullying in adolescents.* Manuscript submitted for publication.

Graham, S., & Juvonen, J. (2001). An attributional approach to peer victimization. In J. Juvonen & S. Graham (Eds.), *Peer harassment in school: The plight of the vulnerable and victimized* (pp. 49–72). New York: Guilford.

Hunter, S. C., & Borg, M. G. (2006). The influence of emotional reaction on help seeking by victims of school bullying. *Educational Psychology, 26*, 813–826.

Kelly, B. M., Schwartz, D., Gorman, A. H., & Nakamoto, J. (2008). Violent victimization in the community and children's subsequent peer rejection: The mediating role of emotion dysregulation. *Journal of Abnormal Psychology, 36*, 175–185.

Kochenderfer-Ladd, B. (2004). Peer victimization: The role of emotions in adaptive and maladaptive coping. *Social Development, 13*, 329–349.

Kochenderfer-Ladd, B., & Ladd, G. W. (2001). Variations in peer victimization: Relation to children's maladjustment. In J. Juvonen & S. Graham (Eds.), *Peer harassment in school: The plight of the vulnerable and victimized* (pp. 25–48). New York: Guilford.

Lazarus, R. S. (2000). Toward better research on stress and coping. *American Psychologist, 55*, 665–673.

Menesini, E., & Nocentini, A. (2008). Comportamenti aggressivi nelle prime esperienze sentimentali in adolescenza. *Giornale Italiano di Psicologia, 2*, 407–434.

Mestre, J. M., Guil, R., Lopes, P., Salovey, P., & Gil-Olarte, P. (2006). Emotional intelligence and social and academic adaptation to school. *Psicothema, 18*, 112–117.

Mora-Merchán, J. A., & Ortega, R. (2007). The new forms of school bullying and violence. In R. Ortega, J. A. Mora-Merchán, & T. Jäger (Eds.), *Acting against schoolbullying and violence. The role of media, local authorities and the Internet* (pp. 7–34). Landau: Verlag Empirische Pädagogik (Retrieved June 10, 2007, from http://www.bullying-in-school.info/uploads/media/e-book_-_Acting_against_school_bullying_and_violence.pdf).

Olweus, D. (1999). Sweden. In P. K. Smith, Y. Morita, J. Junger-Tas, D. Olweus, R. Catalano, & P. Slee (Eds.), *The nature of school bullying: A cross-national perspective* (pp. 7–27). London: Routledge.

Ortega, R., Calmaestra, J., & Mora-Merchán, J. A. (2008). Cyberbullying. *International Journal of Psychology and International Therapy, 8*, 183–192.

Ortega, R., Elipe, P., & Calmaestra, J. (2009). Emociones de agresores y víctimas de cyberbullying: un estudio preliminar en estudiantes de Secundaria. *Ansiedad y Estrés, 15*, 151–165.

Ortega, R., & Mora-Merchán, J. A. (2000). *Violencia escolar. Mito o realidad*. Sevilla: Mergablum.

Ortega, R., & Mora-Merchán, J. A. (2008). Las redes de iguales y el fenómeno del acoso escolar: explorando el esquema dominio-sumisión. *Infancia y Aprendizaje, 31*, 515–528.

Ortega, R., Ortega-Rivera, F. J., & Sánchez, V. (2008). Violencia sexual entre compañeros y violencia en parejas adolescentes. *International Journal of Psychology and Psychological Therapy, 1*, 63–72.

Ortega, R., Sánchez, V., Ortega-Rivera, F. J., & Viejo, C. (2008). Violencia y relaciones de cortejo adolescente. In J. Méndez & M. J. Payo (Eds.), *Convivencia e Igualdade: Dimensións e Retos Educativos* (pp. 11–21). Santiago de Compostela: ICE.

Schwartz, D., Proctor, L. J., & Chien, D. H. (2001). The aggressive victim of bullying: Emotional and behavioural dysregulation as a pathway to victimization by peers. In J. Juvonen & S. Graham (Eds.), *Peer harassment in school: The plight of the vulnerable and victimized* (pp. 147–174). New York: Guilford.

Slonje, R., & Smith, P. K. (2008). Cyberbullying: Another main type of bullying? *Scandinavian Journal of Psychology, 49*, 147–154.

Smith, P. K., Mahdavi, J., Carvalho, M., Fisher, S., Russell, S., & Tippett, N. (2008). Cyberbullying: Its nature and impact in secondary school pupils. *Journal of Child Psychology and Psychiatry, 49*, 376–385.

Smith, P. K., Pepler, D., & Rigby, K. (2004). *Bullying in schools: How successful can interventions be?* United Kingdom: Cambridge University Press.

Solberg, M. E., & Olweus, D. (2003). Prevalence estimation of school bullying with the Olweus bully/victim questionnaire. *Aggressive Behavior, 29*, 239–268.

Thelwall, M. (2008). Social networks, gender and friending: An analysis of MySpace member profiles. *Journal of the American Society for Information Science and Technology, 59*, 1321–1330.

Rosario Ortega

Faculty Science of Education
Av. S. Alberto Magno s/n
14004 Cordoba
Spain
E-mail ed1orrur@uco.es

Traditional Bullying and Cyberbullying

Identification of Risk Groups for Adjustment Problems

Petra Gradinger, Dagmar Strohmeier, and Christiane Spiel

University of Vienna, Austria

Abstract. We investigated the co-occurrence of traditional bullying, cyberbullying, traditional victimization, and cybervictimization, and analyzed whether students belonging to particular groups of bullies (e.g., traditional, cyber, or both), victims (e.g., traditional, cyber, or both), and bully-victims differed regarding adjustment. Seven hundred sixty-one adolescents (49% boys; aged 14–19 years (M = 15.6 years) were surveyed. More students than expected by chance were totally uninvolved, more students were traditional bully-victims, and more students were combined bully-victims (traditional and cyber). The highest risks for poor adjustment (high scores in reactive and instrumental aggression, depressive, and somatic symptoms) were observed in students who were identified as combined bully-victims (traditional and cyber). In addition gender differences were examined.

Keywords: cyberbullying, cybervictimization, adjustment, aggression, configural frequency analysis

Research examining the co-occurrence of traditional bullying, cyberbullying, traditional victimization, and cybervictimization is rather limited. The studies to date (Juvonen & Gross, 2008; Kowalski & Limber, 2007; Li, 2007a, 2007b; Raskauskas & Stoltz, 2007; Slonje & Smith, 2008; Smith et al., 2008; Ybarra & Mitchell, 2004a, 2004b) vary greatly regarding samples, measurement methods, and analytic strategies, and do not systematically combine all forms of bullying and victimization to better understand patterns of co-occurrences.

Ybarra and Mitchell (2004b) investigated online harassment in 1,501 regular Internet users aged 10–17 years in the USA. Online harassment was defined as an intentional and overt act of aggression toward another person online. Fifteen percent of the sample were online harassers, 51% of online harassers were also traditional victims, and 20% were cybervictims. These results suggest a high overlap between online harassment and traditional victimization. It is conceivable that online harassment also co-occurs with traditional harassment in some students. However, the study does not provide information about that.

Slonje and Smith (2008) surveyed 360 adolescents aged 12–20 years in Swedish schools. Cyberbullying was defined as bullying in which the aggression occurs through modern technological devices. Global bullying and victimization were also measured. The global questions on bullying and victimization also included the cyberforms, so "pure" traditional bullying and traditional victimization were indirectly estimated. To recheck the results of Ybarra and Mitchell (2004b) they also analyzed the co-occurrence of traditional victimization and cyberbullying. Subtracting prevalences of cybervictims from global victims, 9% of students were traditional victims. Of these, 10% were cyberbullies. This approach systematically combines three variables, namely cyberbullying, traditional victimization, and cybervictimization. However, because traditional forms of bullying and victimization were not directly measured, results might be biased.

Smith et al. (2008) report data on 533 secondary school students attending Grades 7–11 in England. Cyberbullying was defined as bullying using electronic forms of contact. Traditional bullying and traditional victimization were also investigated. All four variables were considered to investigate co-occurrences. Traditional victims tended to be cybervictims, traditional bullies tended to be cyberbullies, and traditional victims tended to be cyberbullies. For statistical analyses chi-squared tests were applied; this has the limitation that they can only analyze two categorical variables at a time identifying a general pattern of relations. Also they cannot determine which of the cell frequencies are observed more or less often than expected by chance.

Raskauskas and Stoltz (2007) surveyed 84 students aged 14–18 years in the USA. They examined the relations between electronic bullying, traditional bullying, electronic victimization, and traditional victimization; and in particular, whether being a traditional bully or victim predicts being the same in electronic forms, and whether being a traditional victim predicts being a cyberbully. Consistent with the Smith et al. (2008) study, almost all cyberbullies were also traditional bullies and nearly all cybervictims were traditional victims. Again, chi-squared tests were applied. Application of logistic regression analyses indicated that being

DOI: 10.1027/0044-3409.217.4.205

a traditional bully or victim predicted being the same in electronic forms. However, traditional victims were not found to be electronic bullies.

Kowalski, Limber, and Agatston (2008) reported links between traditional bullying, cyberbullying, traditional victimization, and cybervictimization in 3,767 middle school students attending Grades 6–8 in the USA. Based on student's responses to questions about their active and passive involvement in traditional bullying in school, 21% were identified as victims, 13% as bullies, 18% as bully-victims, and 48% as noninvolved students. Bully-victims reported the highest percentages of being at the same time a cybervictim (36%) and a cyberbully (23%). However, the different forms of bully-victim behavior were not fully systematically combined and significance tests were not applied.

The present study analyzes whether certain combinations of bully, victim, and bully-victim behavior occur more or less frequently than expected by chance. Based on the limited evidence on this issue, we expect to find only a very small group of students behaving exclusively as cyberbullies and a very small group of students behaving exclusively as cybervictims.

Adjustment Problems of Cyberbullies and Cybervictims

A large body of research has been conducted on characteristics of traditional bullies, traditional victims, and traditional bully-victims. Being a traditional bully is often associated with externalizing problems like delinquency and aggressive behavior (e.g., Perren & Alsaker, 2006; Veenstra et al., 2005); being a traditional victim is related to internalizing problems like depression and somatic symptoms (e.g., Arseneault et al., 2006; Juvonen, Nishina, & Graham, 2000); and being a traditional bully-victim is linked with both externalizing and internalizing problems (e.g., Haynie et al., 2001; Ivarsson, Broberg, Arvidsson, & Gillberg, 2005).

Only a few studies report adjustment problems of cyberbullies, cybervictims, or cyberbully-victims (Juvonen & Gross, 2008; Kowalski et al., 2008; Raskauskas & Stoltz, 2007; Ybarra & Mitchell, 2004a, 2004b).

Raskauskas and Stoltz (2007) used a qualitative approach and found 93% of cybervictims being negatively affected, reporting sadness, hopelessness, depression, and anxiety. Ybarra and Mitchell (2004b) reported that 39% of online harassers failed in school, 37% showed delinquent behavior, 32% showed frequent substance use, and 16% were highly depressed. Kowalski et al. (2008) descriptively showed that cybervictims only and cyberbully-victims scored high in social anxiety and low in self-esteem. Ybarra and Mitchell (2004a) reported cyberbully-victims executing problem behavior (44%) and experiencing depressive symptoms (16%). Only Juvonen and Gross (2008) controlled for traditional bullying. They examined whether cyberbullying is related to social anxiety over and above traditional bullying using Hierarchical Regression Analysis. While controlling for age and gender, they found traditional as well as cyberbullying independently increasing the levels of social anxiety. However, none of these studies systematically controlled for traditional forms of both bullying and victimization, so results on adjustment outcomes might be biased. It is conceivable that if some students score high on all four variables (traditional and cyberbully-victims) then they will show poorest adjustment.

To summarize, the aims of the present paper are:

(1) To systematically investigate the co-occurrence of traditional bullying, cyberbullying, traditional victimization, and cybervictimization, including analysis of gender differences.
(2) To analyze whether students belonging to particular groups of bullies (e.g., traditional, cyber, or both), victims (e.g., traditional, cyber, and both), and bully-victims differ regarding adjustment; specifically, whether bullygroups will differ on externalizing problems, victimgroups on internalizing problems, and bully-victimgroups on both problems.

Method

Sample and Procedure

This study is part of a larger cross-sectional study of students' social and emotional adjustment. Seven hundred and sixty-one Grade 9 students (392 girls, 367 boys, and 2 unknown gender) in 10 different schools located in Vienna (Austria) participated. The pupils were 14–19 years old ($M = 15.57$; $SD = 0.91$). The sample was highly diverse and represents the population well; 56.6% of the pupils nominated German as mother tongue, with 32 different languages nominated by the remainder.

Participation was voluntary and based on written parental consent. About 95% of eligible pupils participated in the study. Standardized data collection took place about 1 month before the end of the school-year 2007 and lasted about 1 h. The questionnaires were administered by trained research assistants during regular lessons.

Instruments

Cronbach alpha reliabilities are based on the data from this study.

Bullying and Victimization

To measure traditional bullying, cyberbullying, traditional victimization, and cybervictimization we relied on behavior-based items. This is because no exact translation of the term "bullying" exists in German language. The terms which are used in German language (e.g., "sekkieren" and "ärgern") vary regarding their connotations and none of them is fully equivalent with the English term "bullying" (Smith, Cowie, Olafsson, & Liefooghe, 2002). Also, Vaillancourt et al. (2008) found that adolescents underestimate being victimized when a standard "bullying" definition is given.

The response format for all the items ranged from 1 (not at all true) to 2 (somewhat true) and 3 (fairly true) to 4 (very true).

Traditional bullying (α = .79) was measured by a scale developed by Little, Jones, Henrich, and Hawley (2003). This covers six overt forms of repetitive aggressive behavior, for example, "I am somebody who often says mean things to others" (items see Table 1).

Cyberbullying was measured with one newly developed item which covers both mobile phones and computers as means to hurt others. "I am somebody who often uses the mobile phone or the computer to send mean text messages, e-mails, videos, or photos to others."

Traditional victimization (α = .79) was measured by a newly developed scale which comprises the same six overt forms of repetitive aggression experienced as victim as in Little et al. (2003), for example, "I am somebody to whom others often say mean things" (items see Table 1).

Cybervictimization was measured with one newly developed item which covers both mobiles phones and computers as means to be hurt. "I am somebody to whom others often send mean text messages, e-mails, videos, or photos using the mobile phone or the computer."

Adjustment Variables

To gain information about externalizing adjustment problems, reactive and instrumental aggression were measured. The response format for these items ranged from 1 (not at all true) to 4 (very true).

Reactive aggression (α = .80) was measured by the reactive overt aggression scale of six items by Little et al. (2003). To consider the cyberform of reactive aggression one item was added ("If others have angered me, I often use the mobile phone or the computer to send them mean text messages, e-mails, videos, or photos.").

Instrumental aggression (α = .84) was measured by the instrumental overt aggression scale of six items by Little et al. (2003). To consider the cyberform of instrumental aggression one item was added ("To get what I want I often use the mobile phone or the computer to send mean text messages, e-mails, videos, or photos to others.").

To get information about internal adjustment problems, depressive, and somatic symptoms were measured. The response format for these items ranged from 0 (not at all true) to 2 (very true).

Depressive symptoms (α = .81) were measured by seven items from the Youth Self-Report (Achenbach, 1991), for example, "I feel sad, unhappy and depressed."

Somatic symptoms (α = .75) were measured by five items from the Youth Self-Report (Achenbach, 1991), for example, "I have bellyaches and stomach cramps."

Results

We first report whether certain variable patterns resulting from the systematic combination of traditional bullying, cyberbullying, traditional victimization, and cybervictimization occur more or less frequently than expected by chance, by computing contingency tables of ascending complexity

Table 1. Involvement in different forms of bullying and victimization, and gender differences

Forms of bullying/victimization	Overall N = 761 (%)	Boys N = 367 (%)	Girls N = 392 (%)	χ^2	p
Cyberbullying					
...to send mean text messages, e-mails, videos, or photographs with mobile phone or computer	5.3	7.6	3.1	7.92	< .01**
Traditional Bullying					
...to take things from others	11.6	16.6	6.6	18.63	< .01**
...to threaten others	10.5	13.7	7.7	7.17	< .01**
...to put others down	15.3	17.5	13.4	2.46	.12
...to say mean things to others	32.1	34.7	29.7	2.20	.14
...to hit, kick, or punch others	16.1	19	13.6	4.00	.04*
...to quarrel with others	54.7	52.6	56.9	1.41	.23
Cybervictimization					
...is sent mean text messages, e-mails, videos, or photographs with mobile phone or computer	7.1	7.1	7.1	0.001	.98
Traditional Victimization					
...is taken things by others	14.6	17.8	11.8	5.43	.02*
...is threatened by others	10.5	14.2	7.1	10.09	< .01**
...is put down by others	14.4	14.5	14.3	0.01	.93
...is said mean things by others	27.1	28.7	25.5	0.97	.33
...is hit, kicked, or punched by others	7.8	11.8	4.1	15.60	< .01**
...is quarreled by others	29.6	30.2	29.1	0.12	.73

Note. *$p < .05$, **$p < .01$. The overall rates may differ from averaged gender rates because of two missing indications of gender.

and applying Configural Frequency Analyses (CFAs). Then, we analyse whether students belonging to particular groups of bullies (e.g., traditional, cyber, or both), victims (e.g., traditional, cyber, and both), and bully-victims differ regarding adjustment, using MANOVAs.

Co-Occurrence of Traditional Bullying, Cyberbullying, Traditional Victimization, and Cybervictimization

In the first step, bivariate correlations between the four variables were computed. They were quite low, ranging between .24 and .49 (all $p < .01$), indicating that the exclusive consideration of only two variables at a time does not provide sufficient information about the full combination of risk within students. In the second step, we prepared data for the systematical investigation of co-occurrences. To identify bullies and victims the response format of bullying and victimization items had to be dichotomized. Students answering option 1 (not at all true) were considered to be not involved in bullying and victimization. Students answering options 2, 3, and 4 were considered to be involved in bullying and victimization. The percentages of students reported being involved in the different forms of bullying and victimization are shown in Table 1.

Both cyberbullying and cybervictimization are reported comparatively rarely. While more than half of the students (54.7%) reported being involved in quarreling with others, only 7.6% of boys and 3.1% of girls reported being involved in cyberbullying, and only 7.1% of students reported being involved in cybervictimization. To explore gender differences, chi-squared tests were applied for each form of bully and victim behaviors. Boys outperformed girls in cyberbullying as well as in some forms of traditional bullying and victimization (see Table 1).

For further analyses, the items measuring traditional bullying and traditional victimization were aggregated. A student was considered to be a traditional bully if he or she reported to be involved in at least one form of traditional bullying. A student was considered to be a traditional victim if he or she reported to be involved in at least one form of traditional victimization.

Co-Occurrence of Traditional Bullying and Cyberbullying

For this analysis, a contingency table comprising three categorical variables, namely being a traditional bully (no/yes), being a cyberbully (no/yes), and gender (girl/boy) was computed (see Table 2). The systematic combination of these three variables resulted in eight cells. Each cell is characterized by a certain variable pattern (e.g., pattern 222: being a traditional bully, being a cyberbully, and being a boy). To investigate whether certain variable patterns occur more or less often than expected by chance or in other words, whether local relations between these three variables exist, first-order CFA was applied. CFA (Lienert, 1969; von Eye, 2002) is a multivariate method of analysis which checks for local relations in categorical data. Concretely, CFA compares the observed cell frequency with the expected frequency estimated under some chance model. A chance model is contradicted if variable relationships assumed not to exist do exist (for description of methodology and examples see e.g., Spiel & von Eye, 2000; von Eye, Mun, & Bogat, 2008). Variable patterns that are, relative to some expectations, more frequent are termed "types," while less frequent variable patterns are termed "antitypes."

As shown in Table 2, the base model of independence of the three variables was contradicted, $\chi^2 = 15.44$, $df = 4$, $p < .001$, and the existence of one type (pattern 222) and one antitype (pattern 121) was suggested. The pattern 222 indicates that there are more male combined bullies (traditional and cyber) than expected. The pattern 121 indicates that there are fewer female cyberbullies only than expected.

Table 2. Co-occurrence of traditional bullying and cyberbullying: Results of the first-order CFA, Bonferroni adjusted $\alpha = .006$

		Variable patterns	Frequencies		Statistics
Bullygroups	Gender	$B_T B_C G$	Observed	Expected	$p(z)$
No bully	Girl	111	130	126.72	.310
	Boy	112	123	118.64	.254
Cyberbully only	Girl	**121**	**1**	**7.05**	**.005**^{A}
	Boy	122	5	6.60	.244
Traditional bully only	Girl	211	250	244.63	.216
	Boy	212	216	229.02	.028
Combined bully (traditional and cyber)	Girl	221	11	13.61	.187
	Boy	**222**	**23**	**12.74**	**.000**^{T}

Note. Variable patterns represent the systematic combination of three categorical variables: B_T = being a traditional bully (1 = no and 2 = yes), B_C = being a cyberbully (1 = no and 2 = yes), and G = gender (1 = girl and 2 = boy); superscripts mark types (T) and antitypes (A).

Table 3. Co-occurrence of traditional victimization and cybervictimization: Results of the first-order CFA, Bonferroni adjusted $\alpha = .006$

		Variable patterns	Frequencies		Statistics
Victimgroups	Gender	$V_T V_C G$	Observed	Expected	$p(z)$
No victim	Girl	111	198	184.21	.026
	Boy	112	179	172.47	.178
Cybervictim only	Girl	121	**4**	**14.11**	**.001**^{A}
	Boy	122	**3**	**13.21**	**.000**^{A}
Traditional victim only	Girl	211	166	179.90	.025
	Boy	212	162	168.42	.182
Combined victim (traditional and cyber)	Girl	221	**24**	**13.78**	**.001**^{T}
	Boy	222	**23**	**12.90**	**.000**^{T}

Note. Variable patterns represent the systematic combination of three categorical variables: V_T = being a traditional victim (1 = no and 2 = yes), V_C = being a cybervictim (1 = no and 2 = yes), and G = gender (1 = girl and 2 = boy); superscripts mark types (T) and antitypes (A).

Co-Occurrence of Traditional Victimization and Cybervictimization

For this analysis, a contingency table comprising three categorical variables, namely being a traditional victim (no/yes), being a cybervictim (no/yes), and gender (girl/boy), was computed (see Table 3). Again, first-order CFA was applied to check for types and antitypes. The base model of independence between the three variables was contradicted, $\chi^2 = 33.22$, $df = 4$, $p < .001$. Results suggest the existence of two types (patterns 222 and 221) and two antitypes (patterns 122 and 121).

The patterns 222 and 221 indicate that there are more male (222) and more female (221) combined victims (traditional and cyber) than expected. The patterns 122 and 121 indicate that there are fewer male (122) and female (121) cybervictims only than expected.

Co-Occurrence of Traditional Bullying, Cyberbullying, Traditional Victimization, and Cybervictimization

For this analysis, a contingency table comprising four categorical variables, namely being a traditional bully (no/yes), being a cyberbully (no/yes), being a traditional victim (no/yes), and being a cybervictim (no/yes) was computed (see Table 4). The systematic combination of these four variables resulted in 16 cells. Again, first-order CFA was applied to check for types and antitypes. Gender could not be included in the analyses because of very low cell frequencies in some cells (see descriptive information in Table 4). The base model of independence of the four variables was contradicted, $\chi^2 = 139.7$, $df = 9$, $p < .001$. Results suggest the existence of three types (patterns 1111, 2121, and 2222) and three antitypes (patterns 1121, 2111, and 2211).

The pattern 1111 indicates that there are more students than expected who are totally uninvolved, namely no bully and no victim. Pattern 2121 suggests that there are more students than expected who are traditional bully-victims; pattern 2222 reveals that there are more students than expected who are combined bully-victims (traditional and cyber). The three antitypes indicate that there are fewer students than expected being no bully but a traditional victim only (pattern 1121), being traditional bully only but no victim (pattern 2111), and being a combined bully (traditional and cyber) but no victim (pattern 2211).

Adjustment in Bullygroups, Victimgroups, and Bully-Victimgroups

Adjustment in Bullygroups

To check for differences between the four bullygroups (no bully, cyberbully only, traditional bully only, and combined bully) in externalizing adjustment problems a MANOVA with bullygroup as factor and reactive and instrumental aggression as dependent variables was conducted. Gender could not be included in the analyses because of very low frequencies in some cells (see Table 2). Application of a multivariate test using Pillais Criterion revealed a significant effect, $F(6, 1{,}514) = 52.91$, $p < .001$, $\eta^2 = .17$. For the subsequent univariate analyses we used the weighted least square (WLS) method for parameter estimation to adjust for empirical group size differences. One-way ANOVAs showed an effect on *reactive aggression*, $F(3, 757) = 60.70$, $p < .001$, $\eta^2 = .19$, and on *instrumental aggression*, $F(3, 757) = 49.67$, $p < .001$, $\eta^2 = .16$.

Alpha corrected Bonferroni post hoc tests showed that combined bullies (traditional and cyber) scored highest in both reactive and instrumental aggression compared with the other three groups. Mean values and standard deviations (*SD*) are shown in Table 5.

Adjustment in Victimgroups

To check for differences between the four victimgroups (no victim, cybervictim only, traditional victim only, and

Table 4. Co-occurrence of traditional bullying, cyberbullying, traditional victimization, and cybervictimization: Results of the first-order CFA, Bonferroni adjusted $\alpha = .003$

			Variable patterns	Frequencies		Statistics
Bullygroups	Victimgroups	Gender distribution (descriptive information)	$B_T B_C V_T V_C$	Observed	Expected	*p*
No bully	No victim	94 girls; 90 boys	**1111**	**184**	**125.34**	**.000**^{T}
	Cybervictim only	1 girl; 1 boy	1112	2	2.66	.503
	Traditional victim only	29 girls; 29 boys	**1121**	**58**	**109.05**	**.000**^{A}
	Combined victim	6 girls; 3 boys	1122	9	15.96	.043
Cyberbully only	No victim	0 girl; 2 boys	1211	2	2.97	.429
	Cybervictim only	0 girl; 1 boy	1212	1	0.06	.061
	Traditional victim only	0 girl; 1 boy	1221	1	2.59	.270
	Combined victim	1 girl; 1 boy	1222	2	0.38	.056
Traditional bully only	No victim	103 girls; 85 boys	**2111**	**188**	**231.85**	**.000**^{A}
	Cybervictim only	2 girls; 0 boy	2112	3	4.92	.276
	Traditional victim only	132 girls; 117 boys	**2121**	**249**	**201.71**	**.000**^{T}
	Combined victim	13 girls; 14 boys	2122	28	29.52	.435
Combined bully	No victim	1 girl; 2 boys	**2211**	**3**	**16.84**	**.000**^{A}
	Cybervictim only	1 girl; 1 boy	2212	2	0.36	.050
	Traditional victim only	5 girls; 15 boys	2221	20	14.65	.104
	Combined victim	4 girls; 5 boys	**2222**	**9**	**2.14**	**.000**^{T}

Note. Variable patterns represent the systematic combination of four categorical variables: B_T = being a traditional bully (1 = no and 2 = yes), B_C = being a cyberbully (1 = no and 2 = yes), V_T = being a traditional victim (1 = no and 2 = yes), V_C = being a cybervictim (1 = no and 2 = yes); superscripts mark types (T) and antitypes (A).

Table 5. Adjustment in bullygroups and victimgroups

	Reactive aggression	Instrumental aggression
Bullygroups	*M (SD)*	*M (SD)*
No bully	$1.35\ (0.36)_{ad}$	$1.03\ (0.08)_{ad}$
Cyberbully only	$1.43\ (0.30)_{d}$	$1.19\ (0.17)_{d}$
Traditional bully only	$1.76\ (0.53)_{bd}$	$1.18\ (0.30)_{bd}$
Combined bully (traditional and cyber)	$2.27\ (0.80)_{c}$	$1.92\ (0.89)_{c}$
	Depressive symptoms	**Somatic symptoms**
Victimgroups	*M (SD)*	*M (SD)*
No victim	$0.29\ (0.32)_{a}$	$0.48\ (0.44)_{a}$
Cybervictim only	0.51 (0.42)	0.59 (0.41)
Traditional victim only	$0.45\ (0.45)_{b}$	$0.63\ (0.51)_{b}$
Combined victim (traditional and cyber)	$0.80\ (0.58)_{c}$	$0.71\ (0.54)_{bc}$

Note. Standard deviations (*SD*) are reported in parentheses and column mean values with different subscripts are significantly different at least at $p < .05$.

combined victim) in internalizing adjustment problems a MANOVA with victimgroup as factor and depressive and somatic symptoms as dependent variables was conducted. Gender could not be included in the analyses because of very low frequencies in some cells (see Table 3). Application of a multivariate test using Pillais Criterion revealed a significant effect, $F(6, 1{,}506) = 13.89$, $p < .001$, $\eta^2 = .05$. For the subsequent univariate analyses again the WLS method was used. One way ANOVAs showed an effect on *depressive symptoms* $F(3, 753) = 20.16$, $p < .001$, $\eta^2 = .07$, and on *somatic symptoms*, $F(3, 753) = 6.82$, $p < .001$, $\eta^2 = .03$. Alpha corrected Bonferroni post hoc tests revealed that combined victims (traditional and cyber) reported most depressive and somatic symptoms compared with nonvictims. Mean values and *SD* are shown in Table 5.

Adjustment in Bully-Victimgroups

Based on a systematic combination of traditional bullying, cyberbullying, traditional victimization, and cybervictimization and on the results of a first-order CFA (see Table 4), three groups of pupils representing variable patterns that occur more often than expected by chance ("types") were

Table 6. Adjustment in bully-victim groups

Bully-victimgroups	Reactive aggression *M (SD)*	Instrumental aggression *M (SD)*	Depressive symptoms *M (SD)*	Somatic symptoms *M (SD)*
Totally uninvolved students	$1.35\ (0.35)_a$	$1.02\ (0.06)_a$	$0.28\ (0.33)_a$	$0.42\ (0.43)_a$
Traditional bully-victims only	$1.84\ (0.53)_b$	$1.22\ (0.32)_b$	$0.46\ (0.46)_b$	$0.66\ (0.50)_b$
Combined bully-victims (traditional and cyber)	$2.40\ (0.76)_{bc}$	$2.46\ (0.94)_c$	$1.10\ (0.63)_c$	0.86 (0.66)

Note. Standard deviations (*SD*) are reported in parentheses and column mean values with different subscripts are significantly different at least at $p < .05$. Aggression scales range from 1 to 4 and symptom scales range from 0 to 2.

identified: totally uninvolved students, traditional bully-victims, and combined bully-victims. To check for differences between these three groups in internalizing and externalizing adjustment problems a MANOVA with bully-victimgroup as factor and reactive aggression, instrumental aggression, depressive symptoms, and somatic symptoms as dependent variables was conducted. Gender could not be included in the analyses because of very low frequencies in some cells (see descriptive information in Table 4). Application of a multivariate test using Pillais Criterion revealed a significant effect on *bully-victimgroup*, $F(8, 866) = 39.59$, $p < .001$, $\eta^2 = .27$.

For the subsequent univariate analyses the WLS method was used. One-way ANOVAs showed an effect for bully-victimgroup on *reactive aggression*, $F(2, 439) = 70.25$, $p < .001$, $\eta^2 = .24$, *instrumental aggression*, $F(2, 439) = 59.24$, $p < .001$, $\eta^2 = .21$, *depressive symptoms*, $F(2, 435) = 17.34$, $p < .001$, $\eta^2 = .07$, and *somatic symptoms*, $F(2, 435) = 15.48$, $p < .001$, $\eta^2 = .07$. Alpha corrected Bonferroni post hoc tests revealed that combined bully-victims (traditional and cyber) scored higher in instrumental aggression and depressive symptoms compared with totally uninvolved students and traditional bully-victims. Moreover, traditional bully-victims scored higher in reactive and instrumental aggression and depressive and somatic symptoms compared with uninvolved students. Mean values and *SD* are shown in Table 6.

Discussion

The intention of the present study was to systematically examine combined bully and victim behaviors of students and to demonstrate adjustment problems in so far unexplored groups. Before discussing the results in detail, major strengths of the study are outlined. Extending the existing literature, all theoretically possible combinations of traditional bullying, cyberbullying, traditional victimization, cybervictimization, and gender were systematically examined. Accordingly yet unexplored groups of students are investigated. For instance, we were able to identify students who are a cyberbully only, controlling for both traditional bullying and both forms of victimization. Another strength is that we brought to light some combinations of bully and victim behaviors in students that are more or less frequent than expected by chance by using CFA. CFA permits testing each observed cell frequency against expectations, identifying local associations of variables. Independent of absolute cell frequencies variable patterns can be detected, which might have been overlooked descriptively. Finally we were able to compare yet unexplored groups regarding their adjustment problems.

In line with previous studies (Li, 2006; Raskauskas & Stoltz, 2007; Smith et al., 2008) cyberbullying and cybervictimization were found to occur rather infrequently compared with traditional forms. However, in the present sample frequency rates of students involved in cybervictimization (7%) and cyberbullying (5%) were even lower compared with previous findings, ranging between 11% and 49% for cybervictimization and 10% and 22% for cyberbullying. This is an interesting result because we used a rather inclusive criterion to identify cyberbullies and cybervictims. Moreover, in Austria the distribution of mobile phones, computers, and Internet in youth is quite high (Currie et al., 2008; Statistik Austria, 2008) and prevalence rates of traditional bullying and traditional victimization are also high in cross-national comparative studies (Craig & Harel, 2004). The low frequency rates on cyberbullying and cybervictimization might be due to some country-specific characteristics which cannot be determined as long as cross-national studies are lacking.

Looking at the different forms of bully and victim behaviors, gender was an important factor for cyberbullying, but not for cybervictimization. Eight percentage of boys but only 3% of girls reported to have ever sent mean text messages, e-mails, videos, or photographs. Although Li (2006) reported similar gender differences in Canadian 7–9 graders, results on gender are still inconclusive (e.g., Raskauskas & Stoltz, 2007; Slonje & Smith, 2008; Smith et al., 2008; Ybarra, Mitchell, Wolak, & Finkelhor, 2006). In our opinion, gender effects might remain unclear as long as involvement in both forms of bullying and victimization is not simultaneously looked at.

With regard to co-occurrences we extended prior research on relations between traditional bullying and cyberbullying as well as traditional victimization and cybervictimization (e.g., Smith et al., 2008) by also including gender. We found gender to be an important factor when combining traditional bullying and cyberbullying but not when combining traditional victimization and cybervictimization. More students than expected were male combined bullies (traditional and cyber), while fewer students than expected were female cyberbullies. The co-occurrence of traditional bullying and cyberbullying in boys only might be due to the measurement of overt forms of traditional bullying in the present study. Relational forms of traditional bullying were not covered which are more typical for girls than for boys (e.g., Bjorkqvist, Lagerspetz, & Kaukiainen, 1992; Crick & Grotpeter, 1995; Österman, 1999). But Raskauskas and Stoltz (2007) found gender to be unrelated to both overt, relational and cyberforms of bullying and victimization, using logistic regression.

Consistent with previous research (e.g., Raskauskas & Stoltz, 2007; Smith et al., 2008; Ybarra & Mitchell, 2004a) we found that hardly any students are exclusively cybervictims. Instead, most of the cybervictims were at the same time traditional victims. These results highlight the overlapping nature of traditional and cyberforms of victimization. Therefore, to consider traditional victimization and cybervictimization simultaneously is crucial to not bias results.

Moreover, our results indicate that patterns of co-occurrences are even more complex. In considering all four forms, namely traditional and cyberbullying, traditional and cybervictimization, we found students to be overrepresented in some bully-victim groups. Interestingly, students were either traditional bully-victims or combined bully-victims. In contrast few students were found to be a bully-victim displaying their behavior in cyberspace only. In addition, students who were either traditional or combined bullies were rarely not involved in victimization. In line with Raskauskas and Stoltz (2007), and contrary to the hypothesis formulated by Ybarra and Mitchell (2004b), we did not find evidence that traditional victims were also cyberbullies.

To analyse whether so far unexplored groups differ regarding adjustment problems we compared groups of bullies, victims, and bully-victims. We found three groups to be at highest risk for adjustment problems. In a first step, we only looked at bullygroups (not considering victimization) and identified combined bullies to be at highest risk for externalizing adjustment problems. In a second step, we only looked at victimgroups (not considering bullying) and identified combined victims to be at highest risk for internalizing adjustment problems. In a third step, we looked at bully-victim groups and identified combined (traditional as well as cyber) bully-victims to be at highest risk for externalizing as well as internalizing adjustment problems. These results suggest that those students who are involved in multiple forms of bullying and victimization have the most problems. It is important for schools to not overlook these students.

Our research demonstrates how important it is to consider both traditional and cyberforms of bullying and victimization simultaneously to be able to appropriately identify risk groups for poor adjustment. Despite the benefits of our study we also want to discuss some limitations.

Limitations of the Present Study and Suggestions for Further Research

First, we want to focus on the measurement of cyberbullying and cybervictimization. We relied on single item measurements. Although both items comprised all relevant forms of cyberbullying others and of being cybervictimized discussed in the literature (e.g., text messages, e-mails, videos, or photographs) we think these forms should be measured separately in future studies (Smith et al., 2008). The single item measurement might have resulted in a systematic underestimation of frequency rates of involvement in cyberbullying and cybervictimization. Second, because we did not measure indirect or relational forms of traditional bullying and victimization, results concerning gender differences in co-occurrences of traditional and cyberforms of bullying might be biased. Thus, future research should also include relational forms of bullying and victimization to not overlook relevant gender differences. Third, due to low frequencies in the pure cyberforms of bully and victim behaviors we could not include gender in all analyses. Fourth, to determine causal relationships future research should look at cyberbullying and cybervictimization longitudinally. To examine co-occurrences cross-sectionally can only be seen as a first step to understand the complex relationships of variables in students.

References

Achenbach, T. M. (1991). *Manual for the child behavior checklist/4–18 and 1991 profile*. Burlington, VT: University of Vermont, Department of Psychiatry.

Arseneault, L., Walsh, E., Trzesniewski, K., Newcombe, R., Caspi, A., & Moffitt, T. E. (2006). Bullying victimization uniquely contributes to adjustment problems in young children: A nationally representative cohort study. *Pediatrics, 118*, 130–138.

Bjorkqvist, K., Lagerspetz, K., & Kaukiainen, A. (1992). Do girls manipulate and boys fight? Developmental trends in regard to direct and indirect aggression. *Aggressive Behavior, 18*, 117–127.

Craig, W. M., & Harel, Y. (2004). Bullying, physical fighting and victimization. In C. Currie (Ed.), *Health behaviour in school-aged children: A WHO cross national study* (pp. 133–144). Genf: World Health Organization.

Crick, N. R., & Grotpeter, J. K. (1995). Relational aggression, gender, and social-psychological adjustment. *Child Development, 66*, 710–722.

Currie, C., Gabhainn, S., Godeau, E., Roberts, C., Smith, R., Currie, D., et al. (2008). *Inequalities in young people's health. HBSC international report from the 2005/2006 survey*. Copenhagen: World Health Organization.

Haynie, D. L., Nansel, T., Eitel, P., Crump, A. D., Saylor, K., Yu, K., et al. (2001). Bullies, victims, and bully/victims: Distinct groups of at-risk youth. *Journal of Early Adolescence, 21*, 29–49.

Ivarsson, T., Broberg, A. G., Arvidsson, T., & Gillberg, C. (2005). Bullying in adolescence: Psychiatric problems in victims and bullies as measured by the Youth Self Report (YSR) and the Depression Self-Rating Scale (DSRS). *Nordic Journal of Psychiatry, 59*, 365–373.

Juvonen, J., & Gross, E. F. (2008). Extending the school grounds? Bullying experiences in cyberspace. *Journal of School Health, 78*, 496–505.

Juvonen, J., Nishina, A., & Graham, S. (2000). Peer harassment, psychological adjustment, and school functioning in early adolescence. *Journal of Educational Psychology, 92*, 349–359.

Kowalski, R. M., & Limber, S. P. (2007). Electronic bullying among middle school students. *Journal of Adolescent Health, 41*, 22–30.

Kowalski, R. M., Limber, S. P., & Agatston, P. W. (2008). *Cyber bullying: Bullying in the digital age*. Malden, MA: Blackwell.

Li, Q. (2006). Cyberbullying in schools. A research of gender differences. *School Psychology International, 27*, 157–170.

Li, Q. (2007a). Bullying in the new playground: Research into cyberbullying and cyber victimisation. *Australasian Journal of Educational Technology, 23*, 435–454.

Li, Q. (2007b). New bottle but old wine: A research of cyberbullying in schools. *Computers in Human Behavior, 23*, 1777–1791.

Lienert, G. A. (1969). Die "Konfigurenzfrequenzanalyse" als Klassifikationsmethode in der Klinischen Psychologie. [Configural frequency analyses as classification method in clinical psychology]. In M. Irle (Ed.), *Bericht über den 26. Kongress der Deutschen Gesellschaft für Psychologie* [Report on the 26th congress of the German Society for Psychology]. Gottingen: Hogrefe.

Little, T. D., Jones, S. M., Henrich, C. C., & Hawley, P. H. (2003). Disentangling the "whys" from the "whats" of aggressive behavior. *International Journal of Behavioral Development, 27*, 122–133.

Österman, K. (1999). *Developmental trends and sex differences in conflict behavior*. Vasa, Finland: Abo Akademi University Unpublished doctoral dissertation.

Perren, S., & Alsaker, F. D. (2006). Social behavior and peer relationships of victims, bully-victims, and bullies in kindergarten. *Journal of Child Psycholgy and Psychiatry, 47*, 45–57.

Raskauskas, J., & Stoltz, A. D. (2007). Involvement in traditional and electronic bullying among adolescents. *Developmental Psychology, 43*, 564–575.

Slonje, R., & Smith, P. K. (2008). Cyberbullying: Another main type of bullying? *Scandinavian Journal of Psychology, 49*, 147–154.

Smith, P. K., Cowie, H., Olafsson, R. F., & Liefooghe, A. P. D. (2002). Definitions of bullying: A comparison of terms used, and age and gender differences, in a fourteen-country international comparison. *Child Development, 73*, 1119–1133.

Smith, P. K., Mahdavi, J., Carvalho, M., Fisher, S., Russell, S., & Tippett, N. (2008). Cyberbullying: Its nature and impact in secondary school pupils. *Journal of Child Psychology and Psychiatry, 49*, 376–385.

Spiel, C., & von Eye, A. (2000). Application of Configural Frequency Analysis in educational research. *Psychologische Beitrage, 42*, 515–525.

Statistik Austria. (2008). *IKT-Einsatz in Haushalten. Einsatz von Informations- und Kommunikationstechnologien in Haushalten 2008*. Wien: Statistik Austria.

Vaillancourt, T., McDougall, P., Hymel, S., Krygsman, A., Miller, J., Stiver, K., et al. (2008). Bullying: Are researchers and children/youth talking about the same thing? *International Journal of Behavioral Development, 32*, 486–495.

Veenstra, R., Lindenberg, S., Oldehinkel, A. J., De Winter, A. F., Verhulst, F. C., & Ormel, J. (2005). Bullying and victimization in elementary schools: A comparison of bullies, victims, bully/victims, and uninvolved preadolescents. *Developmental Psychology, 41*, 672–682.

von Eye, A. (2002). *Configural Frequency Analysis – Methods, models, and applications*. Mahwah, NJ: Erlbaum.

von Eye, A., Mun, E. Y., & Bogat, G. A. (2008). Temporal patterns of variable relationships in person-oriented research: Longitudinal models of configural frequency analysis. *Developmental Psychology, 44*, 437–445.

Ybarra, M. L., & Mitchell, K. J. (2004a). Online aggressor/targets, aggressors, and targets: A comparison of associated youth characteristics. *Journal of Child Psychology and Psychiatry, 45*, 1308–1316.

Ybarra, M. L., & Mitchell, K. J. (2004b). Youth engaging in online harassment: Associations with caregiver-child relationships, Internet use, and personal characteristics. *Journal of Adolescence, 27*, 319–336.

Ybarra, M. L., Mitchell, K. J., Wolak, J., & Finkelhor, D. (2006). Examining characteristics and associated distress related to Internet harassment: Findings from the second youth Internet safety survey. *Pediatrics, 118*, e1169–e1177.

Petra Gradinger

Faculty of Psychology
University of Vienna
Universitaetsstrasse 7
1010 Vienna
Austria
Tel. +43 1 4277 47375
Fax +43 1 4277 47879
E-mail petra.gradinger@univie.ac.at

Griefing in a Virtual Community

An Exploratory Survey of Second Life Residents

Iain Coyne,[1] Thomas Chesney,[2] Brian Logan,[3] and Neil Madden[3]

[1]Institute of Work, Health, and Organisations, Uk
[2]Nottingham University Business School, Uk
[3]Computer Science All University of Nottingham, UK

Abstract. Building on the research of Chesney, Coyne, Logan, and Madden (2009), this paper examines griefing within the virtual online community of Second Life via an online survey of 86 residents (46% men). Results suggested that griefing was deemed to be an unacceptable, persistent negative behavior which disrupted enjoyment of the environment and which was experienced by 95% of the sample, with 38% classified as frequent victims and 20% classified as perpetrators. No differences emerged in rates between gender (real life and second life), age, and time as a resident in Second Life. A number of self, player- and game-influenced motivations were judged to promote griefing, with respondents overall split on the impact of griefing when compared to traditional bullying. Further, respondents felt that a shared responsibility to control griefing was needed with individuals, residents as a community, and Second Life developers all playing a part. Discussion of the findings in relation to cyber-bullying in general is presented.

Keywords: cyber-bullying, griefing, second life, online community

The prevalence, negative consequences, and antecedents of traditional bullying in schools and workplaces have received a vast amount of research attention. More recently, there has been increasing awareness and emerging research focus on cyber-bullying, which is seen as "An aggressive, intentional act carried out by a group or individual, using electronic forms of contact, repeatedly and over time against a victim who cannot easily defend him- or herself" (Smith et al., 2008, p. 376). However, like many emerging areas there is a lack of agreement on the definition of such a construct and the behaviors underlying it (Rivers & Noret, 2009).

Some elements unique to the cyber-environment may promote bullying behavior; Patchin and Hinduja (2006) suggest a number of such factors. A main one is the notion of the anonymity afforded by the technology; this not only allows the bully to become "invisible" and reduces the risk of being caught, it also means the bully is less conscious of the impact of his or her actions on the target (Slonje & Smith, 2008; Ybarra & Mitchell, 2004). Linked to this, supervision is lacking in cyberspace and there are ineffective formal and informal control mechanisms, especially to monitor phone and e-mail chat. Further, technology can cause an individual to become a perpetual target, as the individual can potentially be faced with the behavior at all times and all places. Finally, power differences in relation to Internet knowledge between bully and target may be seen within cyber-bullying, as bullies are more proficient in using the technology.

As well as the notion of features within the cyber-environment, the impact of cyber-bullying may make this a more psychological form of aggression when compared to traditional bullying, because of the potential to reach a wider audience and the more concrete nature of the written word over the spoken word (Campbell, 2005). Ybarra (2004) found 30% of her sample harassed over the Internet reported being upset by the incident and that depression was significantly related to harassment. Smith et al. (2008) and Slonje and Smith (2008) reported that some forms of cyber-bullying (especially using video-clips) are perceived as having more of a negative impact than traditional bullying, although other forms were perceived as having similar or less impact. Baruch (2005) found no significance difference in workplace outcome measures between traditional or e-mail bullying.

Cyber-Bullying in Virtual Communities

The discussion thus far has highlighted the broader concept of cyber-bullying via e-mail, mobile phones, and the Internet. However, cyber-bullying within online virtual communities is relatively underresearched. A literature has emerged into related concepts such as computer-mediated communication (see Li, 2005 for a review) and especially into the notion of *flaming*. Kayany (1998) defines flaming as:

> ... an uninhibited expression of hostility, such as swearing, calling names, ridiculing and hurling insults towards another person, his/her character, religion, race, intelligence and physical or mental ability (p. 1138).

DOI: 10.1027/0044-3409.217.4.214

Lea, O-Shea, Fung, and Spears (1992) suggest that flaming has been researched within the context of either reduced social cues or the computing subculture within online communication. Reduced social cues theory argues that flaming is a function of the nature of the communication medium itself; face-to-face communication is dependent on social context cues such as nodding in agreement or looking sceptical, but by removing such social cues Internet communication is more "free," social standards will become less important, and behavior will be less inhibited (Joinson, 2003; Kiesler, Siegel, & McGuire, 1984). On the other hand, flaming may be a result of social context, group norms, and a computing subculture (Ybarra, 2004). The social norms of an Internet-savvy group define appropriate online behavior and interactions are guided by this norm. Such norms "are an integral part of the culture of such virtual communities" (Kayany, 1998, p. 1136). Lea et al. (1992) suggest a social influence model where, within online communities, individuals obtain new relationships with people of similar interests that then leads to the development of norms of appropriate online behavior and a culture for the "virtual group."

In an ethnographic study of one of the first avatar communities, the Palace, Suler (1997) identified deviance in cyberspace and suggested that severe deviance can result from offensive avatars (an avatar created with the intention to shock and victimize) or offensive language (indecent language with the aim of antagonizing others). While deviance includes behaviors broader than cyber-bullying, others (e.g., harassing new members and abusing other members) are conceptually closer. Suler (1997) argues that deviance can occur as a result of technical factors (e.g., those who are deviant will find ways to abuse the unique technical features within an online community) or social factors (the standards set by the community of what is acceptable or unacceptable). Further a toxic disinhibition effect emerges where, as a result of perceived anonymity, individuals express themselves more openly in an aggressive and abusive manner (Suler, 2004). This disinhibition effect can emerge from a number of factors including: a perception of invisibility; the asynchronous nature of communication; and dissociating the online persona from real-life persona.

The term more commonly used by residents of online communities to describe more general aggressive behavior is *griefing*. Warner and Raiter (2005) define griefing as: "Intentional harassment of other players ... which utilizes aspects of the game structure or physics in unintended ways to cause distress for other players" (p. 47). Within Massively Multiplayer Online Games (MMOGs), Smith (2004) distinguishes between intra-mechanic conflict (direct consequence of the game rules) and extra-mechanic conflict (consequence of the games being social spaces, which does not emanate directly from the game). He argues that intra-mechanic conflict rarely results in wider griefing activities as it stems from the general spirit of the game, but extra-mechanic conflict is perceived as unwarranted, unfair, and may cause distress. Linking this to cyber-bullying, Smith (2004) suggests that grief play (intentional and severe harassment aimed at causing another person distress) is one type of extra-mechanic conflict found in MMOGs.

One possible reason for grief play emerges from the motivations of those playing the game. Yee (2005) proposed three overarching player motivations: social (the motivation to socialize, collaborate, and form relationships with others), immersion (the motivation to discover, role-play, and escape real life), and achievement (the motivation to enhance power, to dominate and a desire to provoke and annoy other players). It is this latter factor which appears to relate closely to griefing, especially as power is a key element within bullying of all forms. More specifically, Foo and Koivisto (2004) identified four overall motivations for grief play: *Game-influenced* (the protection afforded by anonymity, benefiting at the expense of others; and a belief that the behavior is tolerated or expected), *Player-influenced* (a desire to put other players down (spite), victim vulnerability, and revenge against those who have griefed them), *Griefer-influenced* (a desire to establish and maintain group identity and/or the enhancement and maintenance of reputation), and *Self-influenced* (motivations based on the disposition of the griefer and include need to exert power, need for attention, and enjoyment in disrupting others).

Using an observational study and a series of synchronous virtual focus groups Chesney, Coyne, Logan, and Madden (2009) examined more closely the concept of griefing in Second Life (SL). Second Life (http://secondlife.com) looks as many computer games do – a three-dimensional world where each resident is represented by an avatar (a graphical representation of resident online) – and residents interact with each other via chat, role-play, building, and buying and selling objects. It is also popular – accounting for multiple and dormant registrations – there are an estimated 1 million regular users who spend over 20 million hours logged in per month (Chesney, Chuah, & Hoffmann, in press). Interpretative phenomenological analysis of focus group data produced a series of themes reflecting the nature of griefing, the motives for griefing, and a shared need to control griefing. Specifically, residents saw griefing as behavior that was unacceptable and persistent and which disrupted their ability to enjoy interacting and working in Second Life. Motives for griefing were described as the need to assert power through technical knowledge (especially over those new to the environment), the conflict between seeing Second Life as an online game (and hence adopting gaming norms) or as a place to socialize and work, and the experience of Second Life as a safe environment to grief either due to anonymity afforded to the perpetrator or because the impact on a target is not real. Further, residents felt that a shared responsibility to control cyber-bullying was needed with individuals, residents as a community, and Second Life developers all playing a part.

Overall, related concepts of flaming, cyber-deviance, and griefing have been considered within online communication and virtual environments. The current study aims to advance this area and builds on the work of Chesney et al. (2009) by further exploring the concept of griefing in Second Life via an online survey of Second Life residents. The aim was to explore more widely some of the themes and experiences emerging from the Chesney et al., focus group analysis by examining residents' perceptions of: what griefing is and the extent of it in Second Life, what factors promote this behavior, what impact it may have, and ways to control such behavior. The study further assessed whether the behavior identified here is comparable to the concept of cyber-bullying as seen in the literature so far.

Method

Participants

A private message was sent to 105 individuals accessing two Second Life forums and a request for help was posted on one of the forums. From this, 86 participants responded (46% men from eight different countries [majority in the US]). Average real age was 37.1 years (*SD* = 9.9) and mean time a resident in Second Life was 1.36 years (*SD* = 1.05). Of the 59 residents where data on gender of avatar were collected, 42% stated their avatar was male and 85% of participants classed themselves as relatively or very experienced within online environments.

Materials and Procedure

The online questionnaire was developed from the focus group outcomes in the Chesney et al. (2009) study. A series of closed and open-ended questions were produced to examine the perceptions on what griefing is, the extent of the behavior, what promotes the behavior, and how it can be controlled. Coding was used to analyze open-ended questions, where one researcher coded the responses into broad categories and another checked the grouping. Overall, across all open-ended questions an initial 80% level of coding agreement was obtained and the researchers met to resolve differences in coding to produce a final categorization.

Participants were presented with a definition of griefing derived from the focus group analysis in the Chesney et al. (2009) study:

> Intentional, persistent, unacceptable behaviour that disrupts a resident's ability to enjoy Second Life and which may have negative consequences for residents both in Second Life and First (or Real) life. Mostly, this behaviour is directed at a resident who cannot easily defend him or herself.

They were asked if they agreed with this definition (strongly agree to strongly disagree) and to provide comments. In relation to the definition, participants were then asked to what extent they had been griefed, and had griefed others, in the last 12 months (each day, each week, each month, once, or twice or never). The impact of griefing was measured by asking participants to rate the extent of the impact on the victim when compared to offline bullying on a scale of: "less impact on the victim," "the same impact," "more impact," and "don't know."

Factors that promoted griefing were examined by asking participants to rate 14 statements (shown in Table 2) which related to comments derived from the Chesney et al. (2009) focus groups. Participants were asked to rate (strongly disagree, disagree, in between, agree, and strongly agree) the extent they felt each factor contributed to griefing. Finally, participants provided their opinions on what individuals, residents as a group, and the organization (Linden Laboratory) should do to control griefing.

The British Psychological Society's Guidelines for ethical practice in psychological research online (2007) were used to help draft the ethical framework for the research. Full ethical approval was obtained through a departmental ethical committee process. Linden Laboratory were contacted and we obtained their agreement to collect data and participants were informed before completing the questionnaire about what was involved and how to withdraw if they did not wish to carry on.

Results

Extent and Concept of Griefing

The majority of participants (78%) agreed or strongly agreed that the definition provided reflected the concept of griefing. However analysis of the comments received indicated that many (47%) felt that the notion of "... directed at a resident who cannot easily defend him- or herself" was not correct. The main feeling here was that griefing can be targeted at anyone and not just a powerless resident. Organizations have been the target of griefing behavior and there was a suggestion that some bullies receive more of a "... kudos for griefing someone high profile and harder targets ...." The notion of "persistent behavior" was questioned by 19% of participants, with the thrust here being that a one-off random event could also classify as griefing.

Griefing appears to be fairly common as 95% of our sample of residents had experienced griefing in the last 12 months: 57% only once or twice and 38% more frequently – on a monthly, weekly, or daily basis. Most (80%) had never griefed other residents in the last 12 months; yet 13% stated griefing once or twice and 7% on a monthly, weekly, or daily basis.

For subsequent analysis we defined victim status as those who had experienced griefing in the past 12 months on a frequent basis (monthly or more; 38%) and nonvictim status as those who experienced it "once or twice" or "never" (62%). As few people admitted to engaging in griefing others, the perpetrator category was coded as "never bullied" and "bullied others" (regardless of extent), resulting in 20% of the sample defined as perpetrators (see Table 1).

Table 1. Victim (monthly or more) and perpetrator (at least once) griefing rates within Second Life during the past 12 months

	Gender (RL) (N = 81)		Gender (SL) (N = 59)		SL experience (N = 85)			
	M (37) %	F (44) %	M (25) %	F (34) %	Very (45) %	Relatively (27) %	Little (13) %	Total sample (N = 86) %
Victim	43	34	36	35	44	33	23	38
Nonvictim	57	66	64	65	56	67	77	62
Perpetrator	24	19	20.0	18	20.0	26	8	20
Nonperpetrator	76	81	80.0	82	80.0	74	92	80

Note. Missing data on some demographic variables. Abbreviations: RL, real life and SL, second life.

Demographic Variables

In terms of real-life gender, 43% of the men and 34% of the women were victims; while 24% of the men and 19% of the women had griefed others in the past 12 months. Similar levels were seen for avatar gender with 36% of the male avatars and 35% of the female avatars as victims and 20% of the male avatars and 18% of the female avatars as griefers. However, chi-square analysis to examine gender (both real life and avatar) and online experience differences in relation to victim and perpetrator status showed no significant effects.

Nonsignificant t test values emerged for differences in victim status and age, $t(73) = 0.95$, victim status and length of time a resident in SL t, 80 = 0.73, perpetrator status and age, $t(72) = -1.39$, and perpetrator status and length of time a resident in SL $t(79) = 1.06$.

Impact of Griefing

Half of the sample (51%) felt that griefing has less of an impact on the target when compared to traditional offline bullying; 31% rated it as the same impact and 10% as more of an impact (8% = don't know). Of those who felt griefing had less of an impact, most (53%) focused on the notion of "ability to escape". This essentially revolved around the fact that a resident could just switch off the computer, teleport to another area, or use techniques to escape the perpetrator; something that was seen as more difficult to do in real life. As one resident explained "you can turn off the computer but you can't turn off life or work". Additionally, the virtual nature to Second Life and the lack of a real impact was reported by 30% of those responding.

The 41% of residents who perceived griefing to have the same or more impact than real life felt that the psychological/emotional impact for those immersed within Second Life and who had a strong identification with their avatar was real. Behind the avatar is a real person and this person will experience the emotional reaction to the behavior their avatar was experiencing. Additionally, the suggestion that "bullying is bullying" regardless of the context was suggested by 12%, and disruption of an investment (financial or enjoyment) was also suggested by 12%.

A significant difference emerged in victim status in relation to perceptions of impact, $\chi^2(2) = 7.39$, $p < .05$; 21% of the victim sample but only 4% of the nonvictim sample judged more of an impact and 39% of victims and 65% of nonvictims less of an impact of griefing on the person when compared to offline bullying (for this analysis the "don't know" group was omitted). No significant effects were seen for perpetrator status.

Factors Promoting Griefing

Ratings of agreement for the 14 factors promoting griefing derived from the focus groups are presented in Table 2. The strongest agreement emerged for the notion that the anonymity of the perpetrator may promote griefing. As well as anonymity, participants also tended to agree that a griefer's lack of sensitivity, perception of Second Life as a game, freedom to behave how you want, and perceiving residents as just an avatar may also promote the behavior. There also appeared to be in agreement on a vulnerability element to why griefing occurs (e.g., newbies as easy targets and newbies' inability to defend him- or herself).

In order to examine if gender (real life and avatar), victim status, and bully status related to ratings of motives for griefing, a series of point-biserial correlations were undertaken. Nonsignificant relationships emerged for avatar gender. There were negative relationships between real-life gender and ratings of Linden's inability to control griefing (-0.25, $p < .05$) and residents getting bored (-0.24, $p < .05$); in each case, men tended to agree more strongly than women. Victims tended to agree more strongly than nonvictims (-0.31, $p < .01$) that the culture of Second Life and anonymity of the griefer (-0.22, $p < .05$) promoted griefing. There was a significant negative relationship between bully status and agreement that resident boredom promotes griefing (-0.22, $p < .05$), with those engaging in griefing rating this higher. A significant negative Spearman Rho correlation between online experience and perceptions that Second Life is perceived as a game (-0.26, $p < .05$) was found; those with less experience of online games tended to show higher ratings of agreement than those more experienced in online games. Overall, while there were some significant relationships, perceptions of

Table 2. Mean agreement ratings of the extent that each of 14 factors contributes to griefing ($N = 86$)

Factors	Mean	*SD*
Agree (mean rating of 4)		
Griefers being anonymous in Second Life	4.44	.94
Griefers lack of sensitivity to other residents	4.30	.87
Newbies being easy targets	4.16	.97
Griefers see Second Life as a game	4.12	.91
The freedom to behave how you want	3.69	1.18
A newbie's inability to defend him- or herself effectively	3.67	1.22
Perceiving residents as just an avatar and not someone real	3.62	1.17
In between (mean rating of 3)		
Linden's inability to control griefing	3.47	1.29
Personality clashes between residents	3.44	1.01
Residents getting bored	3.43	1.16
First life frustrations	3.13	1.31
The lack of norms in Second Life which define appropriate behavior	3.00	1.41
Griefers being bullied in First Life	2.84	1.11
Second Life culture promoting griefing	2.59	1.15

Note. Ratings from "1, strongly disagree"; "2, disagree"; "3, in between"; "4, agree"; "5, strongly agree".

motives for griefing were not substantially related to demographic factors.

Controlling Griefing

Analysis of responses to what individuals, residents as a group, and the organization (Linden Laboratory) should do to control griefing was undertaken separately. However, there were common features across the three contexts. Regarding individuals, 23% felt that they should just ignore the behavior as this will not give the perpetrator the attention: "Ignore them if possible. The 'reaction' is probably what they're hoping for." Other responses included reporting the behavior (19%), attending in-world training or courses on how to deal with griefing (19%), using technical fixes to stop the griefing (12%), and banning avatars and sharing their names with others (12%).

Regarding residents as a group, ignoring (14%), banning and sharing avatar names (22%), and reporting behaviors (18%) were all suggested. In addition, 17% of respondents suggested some form of community support: "Already, there are forms of neighbourhood watches springing up in places. Strategies are being put into place to assist groups in being effective in combating this;" while 6% suggested the community should put pressure on Linden Lab to provide controls.

When considering what the organization itself should do, banning avatars was seen as one approach (22%). However, 27% also suggested that Linden Laboratory should provide technical fixes to residents and 7% felt that the organization should provide better customer support: "Hire more in-world customer service staff. Provide some means of reporting immediate issues." Ensuring that consequences for actions are delivered (e.g., "Make repercussions actually work, i.e., actual prosecution") was suggested by 6% of respondents, educating residents on how to control by 7%, and monitoring abuses by 4%. Interestingly, 12% of respondents suggested that the organization need not do anything more than it currently does.

Discussion

Through an online questionnaire, we explored the concept of griefing in an online virtual community and the extent that it mirrors cyber-bullying more generally. Residents experience frequent griefing within Second Life, but the concept appears to be broader than current notions of cyber-bullying more generally. A number of self, player- and game-influenced motivations appear to promote such behavior, but respondents were somewhat split on the impact of griefing when compared to traditional bullying. Results suggest that individuals, residents as a community, and the organization who own the environment have a shared responsibility to control griefing.

Conceptualization and Extent of Griefing

The initial resident-derived conceptualization of griefing from the focus group study (Chesney et al., 2009) characterized griefing as unacceptable and persistent behavior which disrupted residents' ability to enjoy and interact in Second Life. Questionnaire responses showed that the majority of participants agreed with this conceptualization, although the notion of a power imbalance between the target and perpetrator (based on knowledge) was not fully agreed on. Some residents suggested that griefing could be targeted at anyone within Second Life and, while a knowledge-based power element is at work, it does not necessarily mean that a victim is unable to easily defend him- or herself. It may be the case that expert power is a key feature of griefing (as the griefer requires technological knowledge in order to grief) or, as seen in the Chesney study, power may be a key individual motive or drive for griefing. In each of these cases, the victim could be in a less powerful position (e.g., lacking the technical knowledge), but they may still have some knowledge and ability to defend him- or herself against the behavior.

Given this, a revised definition of griefing is proposed based on a combination of resident perspectives from both previous focus group data and responses to the current questionnaire. Griefing can be defined as: "Intentional, persistent and unacceptable behavior that disrupts a resident's ability to enjoy the online environment and which may have negative consequences for the resident. Such behavior tends to be mainly exhibited by those with expert power in the technical features of the online environment."

Even though this definition is not researcher-led, it corresponds well with specific definitions of cyber-bullying (Smith et al., 2008) and Internet harassment (Ybarra & Mitchell, 2004). However, while there are conceptual similarities, it does appear that griefing itself encompasses a broader array of behaviors which are not necessarily specifically targeted at one individual. Indeed, as Chesney et al. (2009) illustrate in the observational component of their study, disruptive behaviors can include harassment, assaults on an avatar, and disclosure of personal information. Therefore, it could be argued that there is a distinction between griefing and cyber-bullying with the former possibly equating to the broader concept of deviance (Suler, 1997) and the latter a subset of griefing behavior.

Another possible difference between griefing and cyber-bullying is the focus on actions being virtual, directed at an avatar and not a person directly. Many forms of cyber-bullying, even though propagated via technology, occur within a real-life environment and target a person directly. In Second Life, griefing occurs solely within a virtual environment where the focus of the behavior is on an avatar or virtual person. Indeed, participants on average agreed that the perception of residents as an avatar and not a real person is a motive for griefing to occur. An interesting notion is whether griefing is actually more strongly related to traditional bullying than cyber-bullying; the argument being that the target is actually seen within the context of the virtual environment and while the visual image is an avatar and not the person directly, there is a closer interaction between target and griefer (as in traditional bullying) than seen in other forms of cyber-bullying (C. Katzer, personal communication, May 27, 2009). It is an interesting notion which requires further investigation, especially in the context of the strength of the relationship an individual has between their virtual and first lives.

Griefing appears to be common within Second Life with 95% of respondents stating they had experienced it, with 38% on a monthly or more basis. Yet, only 20% of questionnaire participants admitted to griefing others, with 7% on a monthly or more basis. These rates are higher than those reported in other cyber-bullying research (Baruch, 2005; Li, 2005; Patchin & Hinduja, 2006), but similar to that found by Hinduja and Patchin (2008). Although, unlike previous research (Rivers & Noret, 2009; Smith et al., 2008; Williams & Guerra, 2007) no significant gender (real life or second life), age, and time as resident effects were seen in relation to victim or perpetrator status. The higher rates seen in this study may be as a result of griefing encapsulating a broader range of behaviors than that considered within other cyber-bullying research or due to the different definitions and classification methods used to identify victims and nonvictims within the area of cyber-bullying (Rivers & Noret, 2009). Within this study, victims were classified if they were exposed to griefing on a monthly or more basis for the past 12 months and as Rivers and Noret show, other studies not only have used different definitions, but have also examined different types (e.g., e-mail and mobile phone) and have employed different criteria (e.g., two or three times, at school, and ever) to create victim groups.

The Impact of Griefing

In comparison to traditional bullying, a half of questionnaire respondents perceived griefing to have less of an impact and 41% the same or more of an impact. Reasons for why it is perceived as less of an impact reflect the notion about Second Life being a "safe" place. Unlike traditional forms of bullying, the target of griefing is able to easily escape the behavior. A resident can turn off their computer, log out, mute the bully, or teleport to another area and they are not necessarily faced with repeated exposure to the behavior as they would be in a school, workplace, or even over the phone or via e-mail. For these residents, because a target can easily escape and because they do not experience real-life consequences, griefing has less of an impact than bullying in real life.

By contrast, griefing can have emotional consequences for individuals in real life, which may depend on how strongly the individual identifies themselves with their avatar. Some residents expressed the view that behind the avatar is a real person and if an avatar is bullied then the person is bullied. As griefing is psychological in nature it may have more of a negative impact on those individuals who have a strong identification with their avatar. These individuals will feel that their avatar is a close representation of their real-life self within online world and that actions directed toward an avatar are directed toward their self. I. Rivers (personal communication, April 27, 2009) suggests that the greater the intersection between the offline and the virtual, the greater the danger of harm being caused. Future research should examine this notion closely to understand the impact of virtual griefing on real-life health outcomes in relation to how strongly an avatar represents a real-life person.

Targets of griefing tended to judge it as having more of an impact than nontargets, which implies that those who have actually experienced griefing have faced real-life negative outcomes as a result of the behavior – in effect providing some initial evidence of the offline effects of online griefing. Yet, the study did not directly question individual health outcomes and further investigations could consider both online and offline consequences of being a target of griefing.

Motives for Griefing

While not mapping exactly that proposed by Foo and Koivisto (2004), on average residents agreed that the self, game, and player- related motives derived from previous focus group research promote engagement in griefing. As with other cyber-bullying research, anonymity, the freedom to behave how you want and the lack of real consequences appear to promote griefing by making Second Life a "safe" environment for the behavior. This may go some way to explaining why the rates of griefing seen were high. Anonymity essentially protects the griefer as no one knows who they are in real life and it allows the individual to become invisible and reduces the risk of being caught (Slonje & Smith, 2008; Ybarra & Mitchell, 2004). Coupled with the notion that griefers see residents as just an avatar and perceptions that griefers lack sensitivity to others, perhaps, as Suler (2004) suggests, a toxic disinhibition effect emerges which may be more pronounced in Second Life as individuals dissociate themselves from their self or reality more than would be the case via e-mail, mobile phone, or Internet chat bullying.

A game-influenced motivation centers on the differing perceptions of the function of Second Life and whether Second Life is a safe environment. Second Life is perceived by some residents as just another online game and these individuals are influenced by the social context and group norms of virtual gaming communities (Kayany, 1998) and may feel that this behavior is tolerated or expected within Second Life. This creates, as Smith (2004) suggests, extra-mechanic conflict with those who view Second Life as a place to work or socialize. Perhaps, as it is not clear what the role of Second Life is yet and as behavioral norms may not be clearly defined, this conflict is likely to continue. Interestingly, Second Life, by its very design, is a role-playing universe, where people experiment with identities and behaviors. People create and act out characters and it could be argued that griefers are simply a component of this game and therefore are an inevitable part of this environment.

Griefers are able to use their knowledge of Second Life and of technology in general in order to cause disruption and harassment to other residents, and this is especially evident when new people join Second Life and lack full knowledge of the system. Indeed the questionnaire data showed that on average participants agreed that new residents are easy targets and are unable to defend themselves. This finding corroborates the Internet-based knowledge power argument by Patchin and Hinduja (2006) and relates to the self influenced grief play motivation proposed by Foo and Koivisto (2004). It is not always the case that a griefer targets a resident who cannot easily defend him- or herself, the power emerges from their proficiency in being able to cause disruption and negative consequences. However, the potential targeting of "newbies" does suggest a victim vulnerability dimension to griefing which is based on experience. Foo and Koivisto (2004) categorize this as a player-influenced motivation, yet arguably targeting new residents is one method by which a griefer can build and maintain a need for power. Although it was suggested that some griefers may actually choose more experienced targets, being new and lacking experience may result in a resident being perceived as an easy target – perhaps as they are not a threat to a griefer's power or self-esteem.

Controlling Griefing

Controlling griefing was seen as a shared responsibility of the organization, the residents as a group, and individual residents. Banning griefers and sharing avatar names was seen as a control mechanism which could be adopted at all levels. An individual can ban a griefer from their own personal area, residents can share names and ban a griefer from a number of sites, and the organization (Linden Laboratory) could ban the griefer from Second Life.

Ignoring the behavior was expressed as a control mechanism for individuals as it deflates potential conflict and does not give the griefer any attention. Arguably, ignoring griefing is easier to do in Second Life than it would be in traditional bullying and other forms of cyber-bullying, as residents can easily remove themselves from the situation. One of the proposed central aspects of cyber-bullying is the perpetual target notion (Patchin & Hinduja, 2006), but in Second Life the target can remove him- or herself from the virtual environment and ignore the behavior. Granted, this will impact on the target's ability to enjoy the online environment, yet it reduces the perpetual nature to the behavior.

Respondents also suggested that individuals and the community should report behaviors and to some extent this does occur through the abuse files facility. In Second Life, residents can file an abuse report if they feel that another avatar violates the community standards. Reports are examined by a Governance Team who decides on the appropriate action to take (e.g., issuing a warning or banning an avatar). However, it was felt by some residents that the organization needed to provide better support facilities and customer support. Reporting may reduce anonymity (in terms of avatar) and increase perceptions of the risk of getting caught.

Linden Laboratory should provide technical features to combat and educate residents on how to stop griefing. This is a more active coping approach and provides the individual with some responsibility in controlling griefing. By upskilling, the resident essentially reduces the technical knowledge power imbalance between him- or herself and the bully and is able to either retaliate or respond effectively. This may reduce what Einarsen (1999) terms predatory bullying behavior; however, it also may increase dispute-related bullying as conflicts spiral out of control.

Overall, our survey has provided some new information on the concept of griefing in Second Life. It is limited by the small, self-selecting sample used, and further research should sample a larger number of residents and control for self-selection in responding. Aspects emerging from this study (such as offline health effects, motives/antecedents, and identification with avatar) need to be explored in more detail using larger samples of Second Life residents. Nevertheless, results from this study triangulate some of the themes identified in the focus group study (Chesney et al., 2009) and suggest some element of consistency.

In conclusion, griefing is seen as an unacceptable, persistent, and intentional behavior which disrupts a resident's ability to enjoy their online experience and may have negative consequences in real life. While some elements may be specific to Second Life, the current research provides insights for researchers examining other forms of cyberbullying as there are clear links with this wider research area. This research is also important as already some commentators (Castronova, 2001) are suggesting that 3D virtual worlds will become the dominant way we will access information over the Internet in the future. If this is the case, consideration of the dark side of these worlds is needed.

Acknowledgments

We acknowledge financial support from Professor Christine Ennew, Deans Fund, University of Nottingham, and wish to express our gratitude to Dr. Andrew Millie, for reading an initial draft of the paper and to two anonymous reviewers for comments on a previous draft.

References

Baruch, Y. (2005). Bullying on the net: Adverse behaviour on e-mail and its impact. *Information and Management, 42*, 361–371.

British Psychological Society (BPS). (2007). *Report of the working party on conducting research on the Internet guidelines for ethical practice in psychological research online*. Leicester: BPS.

Campbell, M. A. (2005). Cyber bullying: An old problem in a new guise? *Australian Journal of Guidance and Counselling, 15*, 68–76.

Castronova, E. (2001). *Virtual worlds: A first-hand account of market and society on the Cyberian*, CESifo Working Paper Series No. 618. Retrieved from http://papers.ssrn.com/sol3/papers.cfm?abstract_id=294828.

Chesney, T., Chuah, S. H., & Hoffmann, R. (in press). Virtual world experimentation: An exploratory study. *Journal of Economic Behavior and Organization*.

Chesney, T., Coyne, I., Logan, B., & Madden, N. (2009). Griefing in virtual worlds: Causes, casualties and coping strategies. *Information Systems Journal*.

Einarsen, S. (1999). The nature and causes of bullying at work. *International Journal of Manpower, 20*, 16–27.

Foo, C. Y., & Koivisto, E. M. I. (2004, December). *Grief player motivations*. Paper presented at the Other Players Conference, Denmark.

Hinduja, S., & Patchin, J. W. (2008). Cyberbullying: An exploratory analysis of factors related to offending and victimization. *Deviant Behavior, 29*, 129–156.

Joinson, A. N. (2003). *Understanding the psychology of Internet behaviour*. New York: Palgrave MacMillan.

Kayany, J. M. (1998). Contexts of uninhibited online behaviour: Flaming in social newsgroups on Usenet. *Journal for the American Society for Information Science, 49*, 1135–1141.

Kiesler, S., Siegel, J., & McGuire, T. W. (1984). Social psychological aspects of computer-mediated communication. *American Psychologist, 39*, 1123–1134.

Lea, M., O'Shea, T., Fung, P., & Spears, R. (1992). "Flaming" in computer-mediated communication: Observations, explanations, implications. In M. Lea (Ed.), *Contexts of computer-mediated communication* (pp. 89–112). New York: Harvester-Wheatsheaf.

Li, Q. (2005). Gender and CMC: A review on conflict and harassment. *Australasian Journal of Educational Technology, 21*, 382–406.

Patchin, J. W., & Hinduja, S. (2006). Bullies move beyond the schoolyard: A preliminary look at cyberbullying. *Youth Violence and Juvenile Justice, 4*, 148–169.

Rivers, I., & Noret, N. (2009). "I h 8 u": Findings from a five-year study of text and e-mail bullying. *British Educational Research Journal*. Advance online publication. doi: 10.1080/01411920903071918.

Slonje, R., & Smith, P. K. (2008). Cyberbullying: Another main type of bullying. *Scandinavian Journal of Psychology, 49*, 147–154.

Smith, J. H. (2004, September). *Playing dirty – Understanding conflicts in multiplayer games*. Paper presented at the 5th annual conference of the Association of Internet Researchers, Sussex.

Smith, P. K., Mahdavi, J., Carvalho, M., Fisher, S., Russell, S., & Tippett, N. (2008). Cyberbullying: Its nature and impact in secondary school pupils. *Journal of Child Psychology and Psychiatry, 49*, 378–385.

Suler, J. (1997). The bad boys of cyberspace. *The psychology of cyberspace* Available: http://users.rider.edu/~suler/psycyber/badboys.html (article orig. pub. 1997).

Suler, J. (2004). The online disinhibition effect. *Cyberpsychology & Behavior, 7*, 321–326.

Warner, D. E., & Raiter, M. (2005). Social context in massively-multiplayer online games (MMOGs): Ethical questions in shared space. *International Review of Information Ethics, 4*, 46–52.

Williams, K. R., & Guerra, N. G. (2007). Prevalence and predictors of internet bullying. *Journal of Adolescent Health, 41*, 14–21.

Ybarra, M. L. (2004). Linkages between depressive symptomatology and Internet harassment among young regular Internet users. *Cyberpsychology & Behaviour, 7*, 247–257.

Ybarra, M. L., & Mitchell, K. J. (2004). Youth engaging in online harassment: Associations with caregiver-child relationships, Internet use, and personal characteristics. *Journal of Adolescence, 27*, 319–336.

Yee, N. (2005). *A model of player motivations*. Retrieved December 6, 2007, from http://www.nickyee.com/daedalus/archives/001298.php.

Dr. Iain Coyne

Institute of Work, Health and Organisations
University of Nottingham
International House
Jubilee Campus
Wollaton Road
Nottingham NG8 1BB
UK
Tel. +44 115 8466639
E-mail iain.coyne@nottingham.ac.uk

Cyberbullying in Germany

What Has Been Done and What Is Going On

Catarina Katzer

Cyberpsychology, Media and Youth Research, Cologne, Germany

In Germany, research on the topic of "cyberbullying" is scarce; here, I review recent work on this topic. The first such study in Germany was by Katzer and Fetchenhauer in 2005 (Katzer, 2005). It was a standardized survey of 1,700 5th to 11th grade students (648 men and 803 women), which mainly focused on analyzing cyberbullying in Internet chatrooms. Because no scale was available for the assessment of cyberbullying in Internet chatrooms at the time, an instrument was developed based on the short version of the Olweus Bully/Victim Questionnaire (Olweus, 1989). Two other studies of cyberbullying were conducted by online questionnaires. Jäger, Fischer, Riebel, and Fluck (2007) surveyed 1,997 students from 1st to 13th grade. Staude-Müller, Bliesener, and Nowak (in press) assessed cyberbullying with data from 1,277 children and adolescents aged 6–22 years.

Because the studies used different methods and measurements a comparison of the results is difficult. Nevertheless all studies made it clear that cyberbullying is an important issue in Germany (Schultze-Krumbholz & Scheithauer, 2008). Katzer and Fetchenhauer found that frequencies for victimization in chatrooms (every few months to daily) range between 5.4% (being blackmailed or put under pressure) and 43.1% (being abused or insulted). Jäger et al. found a frequency of about 20% for cybervictimization in general, with instant messaging the media most frequently used for cyberbullying. Staude-Müller et al. found denigration (22%), insults (20%), and threats (17%) to be the most common forms of cybervictimization in their sample.

Of particular interest was whether bullying is to be viewed as a cross-contextual phenomenon or if cyberbullying has to be seen as a distinct form of bullying. Katzer and Fetchenhauer showed both: on the one hand, there was a correlation between bullying behavior in school and in Internet chatrooms, and also between victimization in school and in Internet chatrooms; most pupils are bullies, or victims, in both environments. On the other hand, 21% of all cyberbullies were only cyberbullies, and 37% of cybervictims were only cybervictims. Of the cyberbullying victims, 47% reported that they just knew their bullies from school, while 34% knew the bullies only from the Internet (their chatroom identity), with 19% knowing them from school and the Internet.

There was some overlap between victim and bully behavior. Victims of cyberbullying in chatrooms showed a tendency to be a bully exclusively in the environment of the victimization (chatrooms), whereas school victims also bullied others in chatrooms. This suggests that cyberbullying behavior may be the consequence of victimization experienced in school and could be interpreted as "fighting back" or "letting off steam."

Hierarchical regression analyses found as risk factors of bullying behavior in chatrooms: a bad parent relationship, high rates of absence in class, high delinquency, positive attitude toward aggression, and a high amount of antisocial online behavior. Risk factors for victimization in chatrooms were low popularity in chatrooms, low self-concept, anxious parental concern, faking the chat identity, and visits to adult or violent chatrooms (Katzer, Fetchenhauer, & Belschak, 2009a, 2009b).

Implications

Many issues for further research are clear.

(1) There is a need for a standardized questionnaire to get representative data about the electronic means for cyberbullying (e-mail, chatrooms, mobile, phones, etc.), the frequencies of cyberbullying, the bully/victims, etc.

(2) Although there is a confirmed overlap of cyberbullying and traditional bullying, there remains a group of pupils who only experience or perpetrate bullying in the electronic context. It seems that mostly cyberbullying is not distinct from traditional bullying and is a cross-contextual phenomenon, but in some cases cyberbullying is distinct from traditional bullying. This hypothesis is supported by the finding that more than a third of the cyberbullying victims knew their aggressors only from the Internet and not from school. In a number of cases, cyberbullying seems not to be related to schoolbullying. Some conceptual differences between cyberbullying and traditional bullying are obvious. By electronic means, the aggressor can hide his or her real personality, which reduces the inhibition level. Maybe this is a reason why it is not only traditional bullies who act as cyberbullies. Furthermore, the virtuality of cyberbullying may reduce the awareness and judgment of the impact that cyberbullying has on the victims. This may encourage individuals to behave

Zeitschrift für Psychologie / Journal of Psychology 2009; Vol. 217(4):222–223
DOI: 10.1027/0044-3409.217.4.222

as a cyberbully who would never show such behavior in a school environment.

(3) The correlation between cybervictimization and cyberbullying behavior allows two possibilities of interpretation. Cyberbullying behavior might be seen as a revenge after an experienced cybervictimization or cybervictimization might be seen as the consequence of being a cyberbully before. Since a number of school victims also act as cyberbullies, further research should examine if cyberbullying has the function of retaliation for traditional victimization.

(4) Concerning the impact of cyberbullying, two other factors have to be mentioned: the possibility of an endless repeated victimization and the large audience. Because nothing that is published on the Internet can be deleted, everything stays forever on the "net," the victims can be confronted during all their life with insulting text messages, photographs, or videoclips in embarassing situations which others have made of them and published in chatrooms or on video-platforms (like Youtube). Furthermore, cyberbullying is mostly a public act, because hundreds or thousands can follow the victimization in chatrooms, online communities, etc. What this means for the impact on the victims should be examined by further research.

(5) There exists a large knowledge gap concerning cyberbullying between researchers, school leaders, teachers, and pupils, so new workshops and trainings for prevention are needed. An important question is how prevention training programs for traditional bullying, like the "Wiener Social Competence – Training" by Atria and Spiel or the "Fairplayer. Manual" used by Scheithauer, can be helpful to prevent cyberbullying. Future research has to examine which new aspects prevention training programs should include.

Research in Progress

(1) Because the research strategies differ greatly in methodology, a comparison of results is very difficult. A working group within COST-Action IS0801 is developing a standardized questionnaire for cyberbullying. The following aspects will be included

- Does cyberbullying occur inside or outside school?
- Are there different electronic means for cyberbullying?
- What is the involvement of individuals in cyberbullying (bully, victim, witness, bystander, etc.)?
- Do cyberbullies always bully the same victims?
- Are cyberbullies and cybervictims known from school or only from the Internet?

(2) In Switzerland frequencies of cyberbullying of 8.8% have been found (S. Perren, personal communication, June, 2009). A working group (Perren, Scheithauer, Katzer, & Schultze-Krumbholz) is planning joint research between Switzerland and Germany. First, the methodologies of completed studies are being compared by checking advantages, disadvantages, and reliabilities, before using a new measurement strategy to carry out a study simultaneously in Switzerland and in Germany. This will clarify differences and similarities in the types of cyberbullying (e-mail, mobilephone, chatrooms, etc.) and frequencies of roles including bully/victims.

(3) In North Rhine-Westphalia, Germany, new concepts for teacher training, focused on the topics of schoolbullying, cyberbullying, and media competence, are at an early developmental stage. Anticyberbullying-training materials will be tested soon by Katzer.

In conclusion, cyberbullying is an important phenomenon in Germany. Research in the future needs networking between the different research groups and should be based on the results and suggestions the first studies have given.

References

Jäger, R. S., Fischer, U., Riebel, J., & Fluck, L. (2007). *Mobbing bei Schülerinnen und Schülern in der Bundesrepublik Deutschland. Eine empirische Untersuchung auf der Grundlage einer Online-Befragung* [Mobbing amongst schoolchildren in Germany. Empirical study based on an online survey]. Zentrum für empirische pädagogische Forschung (ZepF): Universität Koblenz-Landau.

Katzer, C. (2005, November). *Bullying on the Internet: Aggression in chatrooms*. Presentation at the Xth workshop on aggression, Luxemburg.

Katzer, C., Fetchenhauer, D., & Belschak, F. (2009a). Einmal Bully, immer Bully? Ein Vergleich von Chatbullying und Schulbullying aus der Täterperspektive [Once a bully, always a bully? A comparison of chat bullying and school bullying from the perpetrator's perspective]. *Zeitschrift für Entwicklungspsychologie und Pädagogische Psychologie, 41*, 33–44.

Katzer, C., Fetchenhauer, D., & Belschak, F. (2009b). Cyberbullying in chatrooms – who are the victims? *Journal of Media Psychology, 21*, 25–36.

Olweus, D. (1989). *The Olweus Bully/Victim Questionnaire*. Bergen, Norway: Mimeograph.

Schultze-Krumbholz, A., & Scheithauer, H. (2008). Cyberbullying – A problem among students in Germany? Results of a pilot study – need for longitudinal studies on risk and protective factors. Paper presented at the XIIIth workshop on aggression, Potsdam.

Staude-Müller, F., Bliesener, T., & Nowak, N. (2009). Cyberbullying und Opfererfahrungen von Kindern und Jugendlichen im Web 2.0 [Cyberbullying and children's and adolescents' experience of Web 2.0 victimization]. *Kinder und Jugendschutz in Wissenschaft und Praxis, 54*, 42–47.

Dr. Catarina Katzer

Bismarckstrasse 27-29
50672 Cologne
Germany
Tel. +49 221 523066
E-mail nc-katzerca@netcologne.de

Social-Behavioral Correlates of Cyberbullying in a German Student Sample

Anja Schultze-Krumbholz and Herbert Scheithauer

Division of Developmental Science and Applied Developmental Psychology, Freie Universität Berlin, Germany

With almost all German households owning mobile phones (99%), personal or laptop computers (99%), and having Internet access (96%) (MPFS, 2008), electronic media play a central role in children's and adolescents' lives in Germany and also pose a new venue for potentially harmful behavior and experiences such as cyberbullying. Beside first prevalence studies on cyberbullying (Katzer, 2009), there is a lack of studies on risk and protective factors. Impulses for research on this issue can be gained from research on traditional bullying which has shown low scores on empathy to be associated with the status of bully (Jolliffe & Farrington, 2006). Empathy is viewed as the combination of two functionally different aspects: cognitive and affective empathy, with cognitive empathy being the ability to understand another person's emotions (perspective taking) and affective empathy being the affective response to someone else's emotions (Hoffman, 1977).

Sutton, Smith, and Swettenham (1999) hypothesized that (traditional) bullies are able to process social information very accurately and can use it to their advantage rather than being socially "unintelligent" or insensible. Björkqvist, Österman, and Kaukiainen (2000) found that indirect, social, or relational forms of aggression correlate with social intelligence, but not with empathy; indeed, empathy can function as a mitigator between social intelligence ("adequate behaviour for the purpose of achieving desired social goals," op. cit. p. 192) and aggressive behavior.

Here we report findings from a pilot study conducted in July 2007, designed to assess the quality of a number of measurement instruments for application in a later study with a larger sample of students, and to identify characteristics of cyberbullies and cybervictims to be targeted as potential risk and/or protective factors in a future study. We report on (1) the frequency of cyberbullying, also compared to traditional bullying, (2) the overlap between cyberbullying and cybervictimization, and (3) whether students involved in cyberbullying show less empathy and perspective taking and more relational aggression and social intelligence than students not involved.

Method

The sample included 71 students (26 boys and 47 girls) from a 7th, an 8th, and a 10th grade of one secondary school (Gymnasium) in Berlin, Germany. Students were on average aged 14.05 years (SD = 1.20). An anonymous questionnaire was used including self-report and peer-rating instruments and administered during regular school lessons. Students were assured of voluntariness and anonymity before the questionnaires were handed out. They were provided with the definition of bullying from the Olweus Bully/Victim Questionnaire (2000) before answering questions about bullying and cyberbullying.

The Chat Bully and Chat Victim scales developed by Katzer, Fetchenhauer, and Belschak (2009a, 2009b) and the partly revised BVQ (Olweus, 2000) were adapted and extended to bullying using e-mail, mobile phones, and Internet in general ("Internet victim/bully" Cronbach's alpha = .93 and .90, respectively; "mobile phone victim/bully" Cronbach's alpha = .90 and .83, respectively; "e-mail victim/bully" Cronbach's alpha = .92 and .79, respectively). For school victimization and school bullying the partly revised BVQ (Olweus, 2000) was used (Cronbach's alpha = .77 and .45, respectively). The items were treated as single screening items and the bully and victim status was dummy coded.

Empathy, perspective taking, and social intelligence were assessed through the Peer Estimated Empathy of Kaukiainen, Björkqvist, Österman, Lagerspetz, and Forsblom (1995a; German by Scheithauer & Bull, 2006; Cronbach's

Zeitschrift für Psychologie / Journal of Psychology 2009; Vol. 217(4):224–226
DOI: 10.1027/0044-3409.217.4.224

Table 1. Mean values (*SD*s in brackets) and Kolmogorov-Smirnov *z* tests for differences between students involved and students not involved in cyberbullying for (a) empathy ($N = 61$) and (b) relational aggression ($N = 60$)

	Mean values (*SD*)	Most extreme differences (absolute)	Kolmogorov-Smirnov *z* tests	Sig. (1-tailed)	*r*
(a) Empathy					
Cyberbullies versus nonbullies	−1.91 (3.18) 0.20 (4.29)	.46	1.38	$p < .05$	−.25
Cybervictims versus nonvictims	−3.51 (3.75) 0.39 (3.99)	.56	1.55	$p < .01$	−.34
(b) Relational aggression					
Cyberbullies versus nonbullies	1.31 (3.05) −1.20 (3.23)	.41	1.23	$p < .05$	−.28
Cybervictims versus nonvictims	1.45 (2.80) −1.18 (3.26)	.54	1.56	$p < .01$	−.30

alpha = .89), Peer Estimated Social Intelligence of Kaukiainen, Björkqvist, Österman, Lagerspetz, and Forsblom (1995b; German by Scheithauer & Bull, 2006; Cronbach's alpha = .80), and the (self-reporting) Perspective Taking Scale from the Interpersonal Reactivity Index by Davis (1980; German by Kunter, Schümer, Artelt et al., 2002; Cronbach's alpha = .80). Relational aggression was assessed through peer ratings using the Children's Social Behavior Scale by Crick and Grotpeter (1995; German by Scheithauer & Bull, 2006; Cronbach's alpha = .93). Peer-rating scores were *z* standardized within each class.

Results

Frequency of Cyberbullying

In total, 15.5% ($N = 11$) had been victims of cyberbullying, 14.1% were victimized regularly (at least two or three times a month) in the Internet, 5.6% by mobile phone, and 4.2% by e-mail. Some of the students were victimized in more than one way. A total of 16.9% ($N = 12$) identified themselves as cyberbullies, 15.5% by the Internet, 8.5% by mobile phone, and 5.6% by e-mail. Compared to traditional bullying (9.9% victims and 7.0% bullies), cyberbullying was reported more often in this sample.

Overlap Between Cyberbullying and Cybervictimization

Cyberbullies (58.3% ($N = 7$)) also reported being cybervictims. A chi-square (χ^2) analysis indicates that cyberbullies are more often also cybervictims than expected by chance, $\chi^2(1, N = 71) = 20.24, p = .000$.

Social-Behavioral Correlates of Cyberbullying

Differences between students involved in cyberbullying and those not involved were analyzed using Kolmogorov-Smirnov *z* tests, see Table 1. Both victims and bullies showed significantly less empathy than students not involved in cyberbullying. Effect sizes (*r*) show a medium effect for both comparisons. Also, both victims and bullies showed significantly higher levels of relational aggression; effect sizes show a medium effect for both groups. For perspective taking, neither significant differences nor any sizeable effect could be found within this small sample. A small effect was found comparing social intelligence between victims and nonvictims (victims scoring lower, $r = -.13$), but this too was not significant.

Discussion

We found a higher frequency of cyberbullying compared with traditional bullying, and an overlap between cyberbullying and cybervictimization. Also, cyberbullies and cybervictims showed less empathy and higher relational aggression than students not involved in cyberbullying. The small sample size clearly is a strong limitation to the study, and its findings need to be replicated in a larger and more representative sample. Moderator and mediator effects should also be tested for in a larger sample to analyze mitigating effects of empathy on other social-behavioral correlates.

The frequency of traditional bullying in this study was consistent with general prevalence rates found for bullying in German schools (e.g., Lösel, Averbeck, & Bliesener, 1997; Scheithauer, Hayer, & Petermann, 2003). However, previous studies have shown smaller frequency and prevalence rates of cyberbullying in comparison to traditional bullying. The opposite finding of the present study cannot be obviously ascribed to school type, as the school was a "Gymnasium" (grammar secondary school), the school type usually least affected by social-economic factors. However, the high educational level might facilitate more sophisticated forms of bullying including electronic forms. Moreover, girls were overrepresented in our sample, so that more indirect forms of bullying may be more common.

Acknowledgments

This work was supported by the International Max Planck Research School "The life Course Evolutionary and Ontoaenetic Dynamics" (LIFE, www.imprs-life.mpg.de).

References

Björkqvist, K., Österman, K., & Kaukiainen, A. (2000). Social intelligence – empathy = aggression? *Aggression and Violent Behavior, 5*, 191–200.

Crick, N. R., & Grotpeter, J. K. (1995). Relational aggression, gender and social-psychological adjustment. *Child Development, 66*, 710–722.

Davis, M. H. (1980). A multidimensional approach to individual differences in empathy. *JSAS Catalog of Selected Documents in Psychology, 10*, 85.

Hoffman, M. L. (1977). Sex differences in empathy and related behaviors. *Psychological Bulletin, 84*, 712–722.

Jolliffe, D., & Farrington, D. P. (2006). Examining the relationship between low empathy and bullying. *Aggressive Behavior, 32*, 540–550.

Katzer, C. (2009). Cyberbullying in Germany: What has been done and what is going on (this issue).

Katzer, C., Fetchenhauer, D., & Belschak, F. (2009a). Cyberbullying in Internet-chatrooms – Wer sind die Täter? [Cyberbullying in Internet chat rooms – who are the perpetrators?] *Zeitschrift für Entwicklungspsychologie und Pädagogische Psychologie, 41*, 33–44.

Katzer, C., Fetchenhauer, D., & Belschak, F. (2009b). Cyberbullying: Who are the victims? A comparison of victimization in Internet chatrooms and victimization in school. *Journal of Media Psychology: Theories, Methods, and Applications, 21*, 25–36.

Kaukiainen, A., Björkqvist, K., Österman, K., Lagerspetz, K. M. J., & Forsblom, S. (1995a). *Peer Estimated Empathy (PEE)*. Turku, Finland: Department of Psychology, University of Turku.

Kaukiainen, A., Björkqvist, K., Österman, K., Lagerspetz, K. M. J., & Forsblom, S. (1995b). *Peer Estimated Social Intelligence (PESI)*. Turku, Finland: Department of Psychology, University of Turku.

Lösel, F., Averbeck, M., & Bliesener, T. (1997). Gewalt zwischen Schülern der Sekundarstufe: Eine Untersuchung zur Prävalenz und Beziehung zu Allgemeiner Aggressivität und Delinquenz [Violence amongst secondary school pupils: An examination regarding prevalance and relation to general aggressiveness and delinquency]. *Empirische Pädagogik, 11*, 327–349.

Medienpädagogischer Forschungsverbund Südwest (MPFS). (2008). *JIM-Studie 2008 – Jugend, Information, (Multi-) Media: Basisuntersuchung zum Medienumgang 12- bis 19-Jähriger* [YIM study 2008 – youth, information, (multi-) media: Basic research on 12 to 19-year-olds' media handling]. Retrieved 16 Jan, 2008, from http://www.mpfs.de/fileadmin/JIM-pdf08/JIM-Studie_2008.pdf.

Olweus, D. (2000). *Bully/Victim Questionnaire. Partly revised version: HEMIL*. Norway: University of Bergen.

Scheithauer, H., & Bull, H. (2006). *Fragebogen für Lehrer/innen und Sozialpädagogen/innen zur Einschätzung des fairplayer.manuals und zum Projekt "fairplayer" (3. Fassung)* [Teacher and social worker questionnaire on the assessment of the fairplayer.manual accompanying the "fairplayer" project (3rd ed.)]. Bremen, Germany: fairplayer e.V.

Scheithauer, H., Hayer, T., & Petermann, F. (2003). *Bullying unter Schülern: Erscheinungsformen, Risikobedingungen und Interventionskonzepte* [Bullying amongst pupils: Types, risk factors, and intervention concepts]. Göttingen: Hogrefe.

Sutton, J., Smith, P. K., & Swettenham, J. (1999). Social cognition and bullying: Social inadequacy or skilled manipulation? *British Journal of Developmental Psychology, 17*, 435–450.

Anja Schultze-Krumbholz

Department of Educational Science and Psychology
Division of Developmental Science and Applied Developmental Psychology
PF 19
Freie Universität Berlin
Habelschwerdter Allee 45
14195 Berlin
Germany
Tel. + 49 30 838 55593
E-mail anja.schultze-krumbholz@fu-berlin.de

Online Harassment and Cyberbullying in the Czech Republic

Comparison Across Age Groups

Anna Ševčíková and David Šmahel

Institute for Research on Children, Youth, and Family, Faculty of Social Studies, Masaryk University, Brno, Czech Republic

The expansion of spending time on the Internet may be followed by the increased occurrence of aggression to which some Internet users might be subjected. An overt, intentional act of aggression toward another person online is regarded as the manifestation of *online harrassment* (Ybarra & Mitchell, 2004); the term *cyberbullying* differs from online harassment in the requirement for a repetitive pattern of offensive behavior, and a power imbalance, originating from anonymity (Smith et al., 2008; Vandebosh & Van Cleemput, 2008). Online harassment and cyberbullying have been mainly investigated in adolescence (Kowalski & Limber, 2007; Ybarra & Mitchell, 2004); repetitive aggressive attacks on the Internet affect mostly adolescents in middle school and may extend into the high school period (Kowalski & Limber, 2007; Smith et al., 2008). This study aims to explore the frequency of online aggressive acts (as victim and aggressor) through a much wider age range.

Method

The research was part of the World Internet Project (www.worldinternetproject.net), organized by the Center for the Digital Future at USC Annenberg. We present data obtained from a survey done via face-to-face interviews in September 2008, in which the interviewers marked answers in a prepared questionnaire. The basic set of questions was supplemented with questions related to aggressive behavior online, which were used only in the Czech Republic; 1,520 respondents took part, aged 12–88 years. This sample was representative of the Czech population with respect to gender, age, education, region, and place of residence, and quota sampling was used. Data on another 695 respondents aged 12–30 years were gathered later, and this sample was also representative with respect to this age group. Overall, the study comprised 2,215 respondents, with 1,470 of them (66.4%) being Internet users.

Aggressors were identified based on the question: "Have you ever used the Internet to humiliate or harass someone?", and targets of aggressive acts on the question: "Have you ever been mocked, humiliated, or hurt on the Internet?". Possible answers for both items were: "never", "less than several times a year", and "several times a year", "several times a month", and "several times a week". To study the anonymity of relationships between the aggressor and the target, respondents were also asked if they knew their perpetrators or targets in person.

Results

We analyzed the data according to six age groups: Younger and older adolescents, and four age groups of adults. Table 1 shows the percentage responses, by age, for each frequency category of being a target, and an aggressor, of online harassment. We found significant differences according to age in being a target, $\chi^2(20, N = 1{,}465) = 35.7$, $p = .017$ and in being an aggressor, $\chi^2(20, N = 1{,}465) = 34.0$, $p = .026$. Adolescents (12–19 years) and young adults (20–26 years) were more often targets of aggressive behavior compared to older respondents. Surprisingly, the share of targets is somewhat higher again in the age category of 50 years and older. The highest proportion of aggressors is among younger (12–15 years) and then older (16–19 years) adolescents.

It is possible to be both a target, and an aggressor, of online harassment. Table 2 shows the age differences among four roles: "only target", "only aggressor", "both target and aggressor", and "neither target or aggressor". The age differences are significant, $\chi^2(15, N = 1{,}464) = 40.3$, $p \leq .001$). In fact, 0.9% of respondents overall reported being online aggressors only; most aggressors have also been targets. Interestingly, the share of "both target and aggressor" role decreases with age. We can say that groups

DOI: 10.1027/0044-3409.217.4.227

Table 1. Percentages of online targets and aggressors according to age

Age in years	Never (%)	Less than several times a year (%)	Several times a year (%)	Several times a month (%)	Several times a week (%)
Have you ever been mocked, humiliated, or hurt on the Internet?					
12–15 (N = 223)	83.9	9.4	3.1	1.8	1.8
16–19 (N = 249)	79.9	13.3	3.6	1.2	2.0
20–26 (N = 327)	82.3	11.6	4.0	2.1	0
27–35 (N = 309)	90.3	5.5	3.6	0.6	0
36–49 (N = 217)	88.9	6.0	1.4	1.4	2.3
50 and more (N = 140)	85.0	10.0	2.9	1.4	0.7
Total (N = 1,465)	85.1	9.3	3.2	1.4	1.0
Have you ever used the Internet to humiliate or harass someone?					
12–15 (N = 224)	89.7	5.4	2.2	0.4	2.2
16–19 (N = 248)	92.7	4.0	1.2	0.8	1.2
20–26 (N = 327)	95.4	2.8	1.2	0.6	0
27–35 (N = 309)	96.1	2.6	1.0	0.3	0
36–49 (N = 217)	94.5	0.5	1.8	0.9	2.3
50 and more (N = 140)	97.9	0	0.7	0	1.4
Total (N = 1,465)	94.3	2.7	1.4	0.5	1.0

Table 2. Shares of roles in online harassment according to age

Age in years	Only targets (%)	Targets and aggressors (%)	Only aggressors (%)	Not target, not aggressor (%)
12–15 (N = 223)	7.6	8.5	1.8	82.1
16–19 (N = 248)	14.1	6.0	1.2	78.7
20–26 (N = 327)	14.1	3.7	0.9	81.3
27–35 (N = 309)	6.8	2.9	1.0	89.3
36–49 (N = 217)	5.5	5.5	0	88.9
50 and more (N = 140)	12.9	2.1	0	85.0
Total (N = 1,464)	10.1	4.8	0.9	84.2

of victims and aggressors are more disjointed with greater age, with the possible exception of the 36- to 49-year age group, where the proportion in both roles rises again.

We analyzed whether online harassment relationships were anonymous or not, from the perspective of perpetrators and of targets. We found no significant differences between age groups in knowing a target in person from the aggressor perspective. However from the target perspective, 41.4% of adolescents (12–19 years) reported knowing their aggressors in person, compared to only 19.4% of young adults (20–26 years) and 27.1% of older adults (27 and more years). These age differences are significant, χ^2 (2, N = 224) = 9,144, p = .01.

Discussion

This study has a large sample base and spans a wide age range. However the methodological limitation of face-to-face data collection must be acknowledged; respondents may not have felt free in disclosing their aggressive behavior online, which might explain the very low proportion of the aggressor only role in the sample (see Table 2). Given this reservation, the findings show that online aggressive acts probably differ in nature between adolescents and adults. The shared role of being a target/aggressor decreases with age and knowing an aggressor in person also has the same tendency. We can speculate that virtual environments and the real world are more often intertwined for adolescents in comparison to adults, in the perspective of online harassment. It also seems that the Internet empowers mainly young people whose computer skills are more developed in contrast to those of older individuals. Moreover, online harassment has a specific impact on adolescents. It obstructs some adolescents from establishing safe relationships online at a time when peer relationships are crucial for healthy development (Brown, 2004).

Based on the repetitive nature of some aggressive attacks (occurring several times a month or more, see Table 1) and the anonymity of aggressors (Vandebosch & Van Cleemput, 2008), we may speculate that 3.6% of Czech young adolescents and 3.2% of older adolescents have been cyberbullied. Cyberbullying may affect the whole adolescence period. Contrary to the findings of Ybarra and Mitchell (2004), younger adolescents are more likely to be aggressors than older people. We may also hypothesize that the existence of a nonanonymous relationship between a perpetrator and victim and the relevant proportion of victim/aggressor role suggests an interconnection between school bullying and bullying on the Internet. Future research should investigate the overlap of bullying at school and online in the Czech environment.

Acknowledgments

The authors acknowledge the support of the Czech Ministry of Education, Youth and Sports (MSM0021622406 and 1P05ME751) and the Faculty of Social Studies, Masaryk University.

References

Brown, B. B. (2004). Adolescents' relationships with peers. In M. R. Lerner & L. Steinberg (Eds.), *Handbook of adolescent psychology* (2nd ed., pp. 363–394). New Jersey: John Wiley.

Kowalski, R. M., & Limber, S. P. (2007). Electronic bullying among middle school students. *Journal of Adolescent Health, 41*, s22–s30.

Smith, P. K., Mahdavi, J., Carvalho, M., Fisher, S., Russell, S., & Tippett, N. (2008). Cyberbullying: Its nature and impact in secondary school pupils. *Journal of Child Psychology and Psychiatry, 49*, 376–385.

Vandebosch, H., & Van Cleemput, K. (2008). Defining cyberbullying: A qualitative research into the perceptions of youngsters. *CyberPsychology & Behavior, 11*, 499–503.

Ybarra, M. L., & Mitchell, K. J. (2004). Online aggressor/targets, aggressors, and targets: A comparison of associated youth characteristics. *Journal of Child Psychology and Psychiatry, 45*, 1308–1316.

Anna Ševčíková

Faculty of Social Studies
Masaryk University
Joštova 10
602 00 Brno
Czech Republic
Tel. +420 549 49 4393
E-mail asevciko@fss.muni.cz

Cyberbullying Definition and Measurement

Some Critical Considerations

Ersilia Menesini and Annalaura Nocentini

Department of Psychology, University of Florence, Italy

Cyberbullying is reported as an aggressive, intentional act carried out by a group or individual, using electronic forms of contact, repeatedly and over time against a victim who cannot easily defend him or herself (Smith et al., 2008).

This definition implies that cyberbullying is similar to traditional bullying, but involving the use of new communication technologies. Its hostile trait derives from the aggressive nature of the behavior. The intention refers to the degree of awareness of harming others, although we might argue to what extent perpetrators are aware of the seriousness of their acts. The indirect nature of cyberbullying makes it difficult to evaluate the intentional or reactive nature of the attack. Moreover some authors stated that cyberbullying, even if a single individual act, can be circulated widely or copied by others meeting the criteria of repetition and frequently creating an imbalance of power. It is hard to detail the concept of imbalance of power in the cyber context, since in face-to-face bullying it was derived by the higher physical or psychological strength of the bully or by a numeric criterion (the number of bullies in comparison with just one victim). How can we define in the cyber context? Can we refer just to a higher technological ability of the bully or, conversely, to a higher rank position of the bullies in the virtual community?

Wolak, Finkelhor, Mitchell, and Ybarra (2007) and Ybarra and Mitchell (2004), showed that in many cases youth harassed online or by phone were not distressed or could easily block the harasser. The easy termination of these episodes suggests that part of online harassment may not involve imbalance of power in which victims have difficulty defending themselves from aggressors. It also involves other criteria to distinguish between bullying and harassment such as the number of incidents and the degree of reported distress by the victim. In relation to this issue scholars have proposed alternative terms, such as online, cyber, Internet harassment, or attacks (Dooley, Pyżalski, & Cross, 2009; Patchin & Hinduja, 2006; Wolak et al., 2007).

Measurement

Related to the definitional issues there are measurement issues. Research on cyberbullying is growing around the world, focusing on the prevalence of the phenomenon, the relation between traditional and electronic bullying, and on possible correlates or risk behaviors related to cyberbullying (see many papers in this issue). But there has been little focus on the measurement issue of cyberbullying. Indeed in bullying research generally, some scholars have claimed that insufficient concern is paid to psychometric issues in bullying research as well as to the need for more detailed comparison between different methodologies (Card & Hodges, 2008; Chan, Myron, & Crawshaw, 2005).

There are two families of measures frequently used to study traditional bullying and victimization: Normative and ipsative measures (Caspi, 1998; Pellegrini, 2001). Normative measures provide information about what other individuals think of those bullying or being bullied; they measure an individual behavior by asking the perception of others. Peer ratings and peer nominations are clear examples. Ipsative measures provide a personal picture of bullying and victimization, informing us about individuals' perception of their experiences; they are represented by the large class of self-report questionnaires, widely used to measure prevalence of bullying and victimization (Solberg & Olweus, 2003).

As with traditional bullying research, in cyberbullying studies the most used measures have been self-report questionnaires, with key global questions. In other cases, the focus was on types of behavior, such as receiving rude or nasty comments from someone while online, being the target of rumors spread online, or receiving threatening or aggressive comments (Katzer, Fetchenhauer, & Belschak, 2009; Menesini, Calussi, & Nocentini, 2008; Ybarra, Diener-West, & Leaf, 2007).

Given the complex definition of the construct, at present its operationalization is quite difficult. Some critical points are related to the use of global and sometimes unique items to detect the degree of involvement in the role of cyberbullies

Zeitschrift für Psychologie / Journal of Psychology 2009; Vol. 217(4):230–232
DOI: 10.1027/0044-3409.217.4.230

and cybervictims, to the complexity of the definition which can be understood differently among different populations, and to the complexity and accelerated evolution of new technologies which makes any classification often obsolete.

Difficulties with using global key questions on bullying received or perpetrated have been reported in the literature on traditional bullying, including age and cultural differences. Two studies addressing cultural and linguistic differences (Smith, Cowie, Olafsson, & Liefooghe, 2002; Smorti, Menesini, & Smith, 2003) found differences across terms and countries regarding the width of the semantic area of terms for 'bullying' and how close such terms are to its western scientific definition. Monks and Smith (2006) addressed age differences in pupils' and parents' definitions of the term 'bullying', and found that younger children use a broad distinction between aggressive and nonaggressive acts whereas adolescents and adults tend to be more discriminative and concerned about power differences, repetition of actions, and physical and nonphysical acts. Thus, in traditional bullying there are difficulties in relying just on global definition and on the global questions about this behavior. Being aware of methodological difficulties in the traditional bullying area, further efforts are needed to improve our ways of measuring cyberbullying.

Also, in case of self-report methodology, issues related to social desirability of responses can affect the measurement; students may be reluctant to report an act that is socially undesirable such as (cyber) bullying. Studies conducted with Italian adolescents (Menesini, Modena, & Tani, 2009; Menesini, Nocentini, & Fonzi, 2007) showed a lack of consistency between the global key questions and the other statements of involvement in harassing acts. We might speculate that some adolescents hesitate to label themselves as bullies or as victims, while they could claim to have been involved in one or more bullying episodes as actors or as victims. Other studies, although focused on workplace bullying, have reported the same inconsistency between the two measurement strategies (global evaluation vs. single behavior) (Salin, 2001).

Solberg and Olweus (2003) argued that one single item in the case of the Olweus Bully/Victim Questionnaire can be a reliable and economical measure of prevalence. Arguments in favor of a single-item measure are practical reasons related to quicker administration of the measure and lower cost of data processing. From a theoretical perspective, Rossiter (2002) argues that a single-item measure is sufficient if the construct consists of one concrete object that is easily and uniformly imagined.

An alternative strategy to questionnaires and the global questions can be multiple-item scales asking students about the frequency of specific behaviors representing the construct of bullying (Austin & Joseph, 1996; Espelage, Bosworth, & Simon, 2000; Peskin, Tortolero, & Markham, 2006). This can give us a more valid, accurate, and analytical measure as compared to the estimation you can have with a single item. According to Nunnally (1978), multiple-item measures are considered more valid as it is very unlikely that a single-item can fully represent a complex theoretical concept. This multiple-item approach can be more accurate: Single-item measures often lack precision because they cannot discriminate among fine degrees of an attribute. Finally, multiple-item measures can be more reliable: Single-item measures are usually less reliable and more prone to random error. Chance or random error is involved in any type of measurement, however, "this unreliability averages out when scores on numerous items are summed to obtain a total score, which then frequently is highly reliable" (Nunnally, 1978, p. 67).

Some limitations should be taken into account also in the use of multiple-item scales. First, not all possible bullying acts are necessarily included in that list. This problem is related to the theoretical definition of the phenomenon. Second, not all items are necessarily of equal severity: While some of them may occur more regularly without being perceived as bullying, others may have very long-lasting effects even though they occur only occasionally.

Relatively recent statistical methods, such as confirmatory factor analysis (CFA), can help to overcome some of these problems. For instance, this method can evaluate the construct validity by its invariance across different groups (gender, ages, and cultures) and to compare competing measurement models in order to identify the most appropriate score interpretations. CFA enables one to determine whether all the items are equally good representations of the construct or whether some items are better than others through a comparison of three measurement models (parallel, tau-equivalent, and congeneric).

Overall, further theoretically and empirically oriented efforts are needed to overcome some of the difficulties in the area and to try to grasp more directly the meaning of cyber problems for adolescents of the digital era.

References

Austin, S., & Joseph, S. (1996). Assessment of bully/victim problems in 8 to 11 year-olds. *British Journal of Educational Psychology, 66*, 447–456.

Card, N., & Hodges, E. V. E. (2008). Peer victimization among schoolchildren: Correlations, causes, consequences, and considerations in assessment and intervention. *School Psychology Quarterly, 23*, 451–461.

Caspi, A. (1988). Personality development across the life course In N. Eisenberg (Ed.), *Handbook of Child Psychology* (Vol. 3, pp. 311–388). New York: Wiley.

Chan, J. H. F., Myron, R., & Crawshaw, M. (2005). The efficacy of non-anonymous measures of bullying. *School Psychology International, 26*, 443–458.

Dooley, J. J., Pyżalski, J., & Cross, D. (1996). Cyberbullying versus face-to-face bullying: A theoretical and conceptual review. *Zeitschrift für Psychologie / Journal of Psychology, 214*(4), 182–188.

Espelage, D. L., Bosworth, K., & Simon, T. R. (2000). Examining the social context of bullying behaviors in early adolescence. *Journal of Counseling and Development, 78*, 326–333.

Katzer, C., Fetchenhauer, D., & Belschak, F. (2009). Cyberbullying: Who are the victims?: A comparison of victimization in Internet chatrooms and victimization in school. *Journal of Media Psychology: Theories, Methods, and Applications, 21*, 25–36.

Menesini, E., Calussi, P., & Nocentini, A. (2008). *Cyber Bullying and Psychological Health Symptoms*. Poster Workshop, XXth ISSBD Conference, Würzburg, Germany.

Menesini, E., Modena, M., & Tani, F. (2009). Bullying and victimization in adolescence. Concurrent and stable roles and psychological health symptoms. *Journal of Genetic Psychology, 2*, 115–134.

Menesini, E., Nocentini, A., & Fonzi, A. (2007). Analisi longitudinale e differenze di genere nei comportamenti aggressivi in adolescenza [Longitudinal and differential analysis of gender in aggressive behaviors during adolescence]. *Età Evolutiva, 87*, 78–85.

Monks, C. P., & Smith, P. K. (2006). Definitions of 'bullying': Age differences in understanding of the term, and the role of experience. *British Journal of Developmental Psychology, 24*, 801–821.

Nunnally, J. C. (1978). *Psychometric Theory.* New York: McGraw-Hill.

Patchin, J. W., & Hinduja, S. (2006). Bullies move beyond the schoolyard. A preliminary look at cyberbullying. *Youth Violence and Juvenile Justice, 4*, 148–169.

Pellegrini, A. D. (2001). Sampling instances of victimization in middle school. In J. Juvonen & S. Graham (Eds.), *Peer Harassment in School* (pp. 125–144). New York: Guildford Press.

Peskin, M. F., Tortolero, S. R., & Markham, C. M. (2006). Bullying and victimization among Black and Hispanic adolescents. *Adolescence, 41*(163), 467–484.

Rossiter, J. R. (2002). The C-OAR-SE procedure for scale development in marketing. *International Journal of Research in Marketing, 19*, 305–335.

Salin, D. (2001). Prevalence and forms of bullying among business professionals: A comparison of two different strategies for measuring bullying. *European Journal of Work and Organizational Psychology, 10*, 425–441.

Smith, P. K., Cowie, H., Olafsson, R., & Liefooghe, A. M. (2002). Definition of bullying: A comparison of terms used, and age and sex differences, in a 14-country international comparison. *Child Development, 73*, 1119–1133.

Smith, P. K., Mahdavi, J., Carvalho, M., Fisher, S., Russell, S., & Tippett, N. (2008). Cyberbullying: Its nature and impact in secondary school pupils. *Journal of Child Psychology and Psychiatry, 49*, 376–385.

Smorti, A., Menesini, E., & Smith, P. K. (2003). Parents' definition of children's bullying in a five-country comparison. *Journal of Cross-Cultural Psychology, 34*, 417–432.

Solberg, M., & Olweus, D. (2003). Prevalence estimation of school bullying with the Olweus Bully/Victim Questionnaire. *Aggressive Behaviour, 29*, 239–268.

Wolak, J., Finkelhor, D., Mitchell, K. J., & Ybarra, M. J. (2007). Online "predators" and their victims. Myths, realities, and implications for prevention and treatment. *American Psychologist, 63*, 111–128.

Ybarra, M. L., Diener-West, M., & Leaf, P. J. (2007). Examining the overlap in Internet harassment and school bullying: Implications for school intervention. *Journal of Adolescent Health, 41*, S42–S50.

Ybarra, M. L., & Mitchell, K. J. (2004). Online aggressor/targets, aggressor and targets: A comparison of associated youth characteristics. *Journal of Child Psychology and Psychiatry, 45*, 1308–1316.

Ersilia Menesini

Department of Psychology
Via di San Salvi
12 50135 Florence
Italy
Tel. +39 055 623-7836
E-mail menesini@psico.unifi.it

European Project on Bullying and Cyberbullying Granted by Daphne II Programme

Maria Luisa Genta, Antonella Brighi, and Annalisa Guarini
Department of Psychology, University of Bologna, Italy

Daphne II (2004–2008) is a very wide program which aims at supporting organizations that develop measures and actions to prevent or to combat all types of violence against children, young people, and women, and to protect the victims and groups at risk.

One project granted by the Daphne II programme from February 2007 to February 2009 was: "An investigation into forms of peer-peer bullying at school in preadolescent and adolescent groups: new instruments and preventing strategies". This has been coordinated by an Italian group (Genta, Brighi, and Guarini, University of Bologna) involving different European Countries (English group: Smith, Thompson, and Tippett, Goldsmiths, University of London; Spanish group: Ortega, Mora-Merchan, and Calmaestra, University of Cordoba; Finnish group: Salmivalli and Pöyhönen, University of Turku; and second Italian group: Buccoliero and Promeco-Ferrara) and a nonEuropean Country as an associate partner (Bosnia-Herzegovina group: Canevaro, Malaguti, and Tomic, University of Bologna and Hatibovic, University of Tuzla).

This project aimed at investigating forms of school bullying and cyberbullying and the social dynamics in 12–16-year-old boys and girls, with a particular emphasis on cyberbullying, and their impact on prosocial peer-peer strategies, as well as on the nature and predictors of bystanding and defending behaviors toward victimized peers. The project consisted of three main activities:

(1) Creation of new tools for assessing bullying, cyberbullying, and aggressive dynamics in the peer group and examination of the impact of forms of prosocial behavior and participant roles (Genta, Berdondini, Brighi, & Guarini, 2009). The international team has jointly created a new questionnaire which focuses on four main types of bullying (direct bullying, indirect bullying, bullying via mobile, and bullying via Internet) and the reactions of victims and bystanders, together with questions about school climate (perception of safety and well-being at school, quality of relationships among peers and peers-adults). The questionnaire includes questions on feelings of loneliness, and perceived self-esteem, and adopting revised and shortened versions of validated questionnaires (Melotti, Corsano, & Scarpuzzi, 2006).

(2) Comparison among data collected in different countries with the same theoretical and methodological background. After a piloting phase in each of the countries, the researchers collected a total sample of 6,500 students, from three age levels: 12–13; 14–15; and 16–17 years from equivalent school levels.

(3) Preparation of specific educational materials in order to increase the awareness of teachers, parents, and policymakers on cyberbullying: educational videos on bullying and cyberbullying, printed materials like leaflets and pamphlets, books (Genta, Brighi, & Guarini, 2009), and activation of a website (www.bullyingandcyber.net); a public information campaign open to all the citizens disseminating the results of the study.

The research has established that forms of cyberbullying are Europe wide, with high percentages especially in those countries where a global and systematic policy is still lacking (i.e., Italy and Bosnia-Herzegovina), pointing out the necessity to create shared national guidelines for intervention and for devising projects for teacher training. In parallel, it seems urgent to involve parents too in actions of sensitization on bullying and cyberbullying, the latter an underestimated problem by parents.

The research teams are now involved in their own countries, to devise intervention strategies tailored to specific cultural contexts. For this objective, good suggestions will come also from qualitative data, which were collected in Italy and Bosnia-Herzegovina using focus group methodology, with content analysis of the videotaped sessions. Parallel to researchers' activity, our project has involved teachers and schools, through a research-action process, in a deep evaluation of their educational choices and organizational processes in order to deal with bullying and cyberbullying.

References

Genta, M. L., Berdondini, L., Brighi, A., & Guarini, A. (2009). Il fenomeno del bullismo elettronico in adolescenza. *Rassegna di Psicologia, XXVI*, 141–161.

Genta, M. L., Brighi, A., & Guarini, A. (2009). *Bullismo elettronico: fattori di rischio connessi alle nuove tecnologie.* Roma: Carocci.

Melotti, G., Corsano, P., & Scarpuzzi, P. (2006). An Italian application of the Louvain loneliness scale for children and adolescents (LLCA). *TPM Testing, Psicometria e Metodologia, 13*, 237–255.

Maria Luisa Genta

Dipartimento di Psicologia
Viale Berti Pichat 5
40127 Bologna
Italy
E-mail marialuisa.genta@unibo.it

DOI: 10.1027/0044-3409.217.4.233

CyberTraining: A Research-Based European Training Manual on Cyberbullying

Thomas Jäger
Center for Educational Research, University of Koblenz-Landau, Germany

The CyberTraining project is an EU-funded project supported by the Leonardo da Vinci/Lifelong Learning Programme of the European Commission. The 2-year project that started in late 2008 aims to provide a training manual on cyberbullying for trainers dealing with different target groups such as pupils, parents, teachers, or whole schools. The CyberTraining project is a joint initiative of the Anti-Bullying Centre, Trinity College, Dublin, Ireland; the Universities of Seville, Cordoba, and Madrid, Spain; the Faculty of Psychology and Educational Sciences, University of Coimbra, Portugal; the University of Surrey, United Kingdom; Infoart, Bulgaria, and Ynternet, Switzerland, coordinated by the Zentrum für empirische pädagogische Forschung, ZepF; University of Koblenz-Landau, Germany.

The training manual will include background information on cyberbullying, its nature and extent in Europe, current projects, initiatives and approaches tackling the cyberbullying problem, best practice Europe wide as well as practical guidance and resources for trainers working with the target groups of pupils, parents, teachers, and schools. The training manual aims at being well grounded on the latest research outcomes on cyberbullying as well as experiences and evaluation outcomes related to initiatives that tackle the cyberbullying problem from various perspectives. This will ensure that professionals have the opportunity to base their work on high-quality resources that reflect the state-of-the-art in terms of cyberbullying. The manual will be practice oriented and aims to prepare trainers for work with different target groups. It will be made available online in form of a user-friendly e-Book in English, German, Spanish, French, and Portuguese versions.

The CyberTraining project will approach the cyberbullying problem from a European perspective by analyzing initiatives from throughout Europe. The trainers and other professionals can profit from experiences that have been gained in other parts of Europe. This would promote the realization of a common European approach in the field where there is less national experience than in other fields.

In its first phase the project puts a specific emphasis on involving the target group of trainers as well as experts on cyberbullying in the process of developing the manual. The development of the training manual will build on a multi-level research process that starts with an initial analysis of trainers' needs and preferences in terms of a training manual as well as a multi-level qualitative questioning process that aims at structuring experts' views on the cyberbullying problem.

Basing on the outcomes of the trainers and the experts questioning the partners will continue with target-oriented research on the nature and extent of the cyberbullying problem and approaches that tackle the cyberbullying problem and best practice in the field. The partners' research outcomes will be summarized in national reports that together with transnational comparative analysis will be compiled in transnational reports. In order not to focus on the situation in the project's partner countries alone it is envisaged to invite researchers from across Europe to submit articles on the situation in their countries that will be published in form of a book as well as an e-Book.

For further information, please see http://www.cyber-training-project.org.

Thomas Jäger

Center for Educational Research
University of Koblenz-Landau
Bürgerstraße 23
76829 Landau
Germany
Tel. +49 6341 906187
Fax +49 6341 906166
E-mail jaegerth@zepf.uni-landau.de

Research on Cyberbullying in Belgium, and Internet Rights Observatory Advice

Michel Walrave
University of Antwerp, Belgium

Public authorities in Belgium have undertaken steps to develop research-based anticyberbullying actions. As a first initiative, the Institute Society and Technology at the request of the Commission for Culture, Youth, Sport, and the Media of the Flemish Parliament financed a study about cyberbullying. The aim was to gather data about the prevalence of cyberbullying among youngsters and about the profile of bullies and victims. The study was conducted in October 2005 by researchers from the University of Antwerp (Vandebosch, Van Cleemput, Mortelmans, & Walrave, 2006; Vandebosch & Van Cleemput, 2009). A total of 636 primary schoolchildren and 1,416 secondary school students participated in a classroom survey. The results of this survey are summarized in a research report (http://www.samenlevingentechnologie.be).

The second initiative fits within the framework of the TIRO project (Teens & ICT: risks and opportunities, http://www.ua.ac.be/tiro). This research was financed by the Belgian Science Policy (research program Society and Future) and was a collaboration between the Universities of Brussels (SMIT-VUB), Namur (CRID and CITA FUNDP), and Antwerp (MIOS-University of Antwerp). A survey, including cyberbullying, was conducted by researchers of the University of Antwerp among 1,318 pupils (12–18 year olds) and 571 parents concerning the opportunities and the risks linked with Internet use (Walrave, Lenaerts, & De Moor, 2008; Heirman & Walrave, 2008; Walrave & Heirman, 2009).

The data from these projects were integrated in a publication in Dutch and French (Walrave, Demoulin, Heirman, & Van de Perre, 2009), that formed the basis of the Internet Rights Observatory's policy advice on cyberbullying. This advice is a third important step taken by the Internet Rights Observatory, an independent think tank associated with the Belgian Federal Public Service Economy. The Observatory is a multistakeholder organization, supported by the Federal Public Service Economy, that drafts advice and sensitizes Internet users and organizations on different Internet-related issues. Research teams of the Universities of Namur and Antwerp support the members of the Observatory with scientific research and assist them in their different missions.

On the Safer Internet Day (February 10, 2009) the Observatory presented the new advice on cyberbullying, together with a research report, and guidelines for parents, teachers, children, and teenagers. This information can be downloaded (in French and Dutch) from the Observatory's website (http://www.internet-observatory.be). The policy advice stresses the following topics:

(1) The development of educational programs, focusing on media literacy.
(2) The involvement of mass media in informing and sensitizing the public.
(3) The development of a uniform prevention program for all types of bullying, taking the specificity of cyberbullying into account.
(4) Creating increased vigilance of educators and parents for cyberbullying in lower secondary education (age 12–15 years).
(5) The development of a "Whole School Community" approach for (cyber)bullying.
(6) Creating awareness of the mitigating effects of elevated parental supervision.
(7) Prevention efforts are preferable to sanctioning approaches.

References

Heirman, W., & Walrave, M. (2008). Assessing concerns and issues about the mediation of technology in cyberbullying. *Cyberpsychology: Journal of Psychosocial Research on Cyberspace, 2*(2), Retrieved from http://www.cyberpsychology.eu/view.php?cisloclanku=2008111401&article=1.

Vandebosch, H., Van Cleemput, K., Mortelmans, D., & Walrave, M. (2006). *Cyberpesten bij jongeren in Vlaanderen, Studie in opdracht van het viWTA – Samenleving & Technologie.* Available: http://www.samenlevingentechnologie.be/ists/nl/publicaties/rapporten/rapport_cyberpesten.html.

Vandebosch, H., & Van Cleemput, K. (2009). Cyber bullying among youngsters: Prevalence and profile of bullies and victims. *New Media & Society, 11*(8), 1–23.

Walrave, M., Demoulin, M., Heirman, W., & Van de Perre, A. (2009). *Cyberpesten: pesten in bits & bytes. Observatorium van de Rechten op het Internet/Cyberharcèlement: Risque du virtuel, impact dans le réel* Observatoire des Droits de l'Internet. Available: http://www.internet-observatory.be/.

Walrave, M., & Heirman, W. (2009). Cyberbullying: predicting victimization and perpetration. *Children & Society: The International Journal of Childhood and Children's Services.* Advance online publication. doi 10.1111/j.1099-0860.2009.00260.x.

Walrave, M., Lenaerts, S., & De Moor, S. (2008). *Cyberteens @ risk? Tieners verknocht aan internet, maar ook waakzaam voor risico's? Synthese survey, focusgroepen en brainstormsessies* BELSPO – UA. Available: http://www.ua.ac.be/tiro.

Michel Walrave

Department of Communication Studies
University of Antwerp
Sint Jacobstraat 2
2000 Antwerp
Belgium
E-mail michel.walrave@ua.ac.be;
Website www.ua.ac.be/mios; www.ua.ac.be/cyberbullying

COST Action IS0801 on Cyberbullying

Peter K. Smith and Ruth Sittichai

Department of Psychology, Goldsmiths, University of London, UK

COST is an intergovernmental framework for European Cooperation in Science and Technology, allowing the coordination of nationally funded research on a European level. COST contributes to reducing the fragmentation in European research investments and opening the European Research Area to cooperation worldwide. COST does not fund original research, but it does fund a range of networking and dissemination opportunities. These include: management meetings; scientific workshops and seminars; short-term scientific missions; training schools; and publications. Some priority is given to helping Early Stage Researchers (within 10 years of their doctoral or last relevant degree).

COST IS0801: *Cyberbullying: Coping with negative and enhancing positive uses of new technologies, in relationships in educational settings,* is in the Individuals, Societies, Cultures and Health (ISCH) domain. It started in late October 2008 and continues for 4 years. The Chair of the Action is Professor Peter K. Smith (p.smith@gold.ac.uk); the Vice-Chair is Professor Georges Steffgen (georges.steffgen@uni.lu). The COST Secretariat is currently Ms. Ruth Sittichai (pss02rs@gold.ac.uk).

What Is This COST Action About?

Researchers, pupils, parents, teachers, unions, and local, regional, and national authorities are all in various ways grappling with the issues involved in cyberbullying, in consultation with mobile phone companies and Internet service providers. The more detailed objectives of COST IS0801 are:

- Sharing of developing expertise in knowledge base and measurement techniques across researchers.
- Sharing of input from outside the research community; specifically, from legal experts; and from mobile phone companies and Internet service providers.

- Sharing of already nationally published guidelines, and recommended coping strategies, in different countries, including positive uses of new technologies in the relationship areas; moving toward a common set of guidelines applicable for the European Community.
- Increased awareness of the issue, and of the outcomes of the Action, to likely beneficiaries of the Action.

To date (October 2009) the Action has 25 participating COST countries (Austria, Belgium, Bulgaria, Czech Republic, Denmark, Finland, Germany, Greece, Hungary, Iceland, Ireland, Israel, Italy, Latvia, Lithuania, Luxembourg, The Netherlands, Norway, Poland, Portugal, Spain, Sweden, Switzerland, Turkey, and United Kingdom), plus non-COST participation from four institutions in Australia and one in Ukraine. Altogether 61 persons are on the Management Committee (MC). It is still possible for other countries to join the Action and for other persons to join the MC.

Working Groups

Much of the activity is managed by Working Groups (WGs), made up from members of the MC. There are six WGs in this Action:

- WG1: Co-ordinator: *Professor Ersilia Menesini*, menesini @psico.unifi.it.

Sharing of developing expertise in knowledge base and measurement techniques across researchers; organisation of Workshop 1.

- WG2: Co-ordinator: *Dr. Iain Coyne*, Iain.Coyne@ nottingham.ac.uk.

Sharing of input from outside the research community; specifically, from legal experts and from mobile phone companies and internet service providers; organisation of Workshop 2.

- WG3: Co-ordinator: *Professor Maritta Valimaki*, mava@ utu.fi.

Sharing of already nationally published guidelines, and recommended coping strategies, in different countries, including positive uses of new technologies in the relationships area; organisation of Workshop 3.

- WG4: Co-ordinator: *Dr. Vera Boronenko*, vera boronenko@ inbox.lv.

Actively initiate and organise short exchanges, co-supervision of students, and any additional small workshops or meetings that may be necessary.

- WG5: Co-ordinator: *Professor Sonja Perren*, perren@ jacobscenter.uzh.ch.

Sharing of research on coping strategies, in different countries, and of research that will inform the work on guidelines carried out by WG3.

- WG6: Co-ordinator: *Professor Angela Costabile*, a.costa bile@unical.it.

Positive uses of new technologies, in relationships in educational settings.

Workshops and Conferences

The first major Workshop of the Action was held in Vilnius, Lithuania, 22–23 August 2009. The theme was: "Cyber bullying: definition and measurement issues". Keynote speakers included Peter Smith (UK), Michele Ybarra (USA), Phillip Slee (Australia), and Donna Cross (Australia). In preparation are Workshop 2, in Antwerp, 26 May 2010: Sharing of input from outside the research community; Workshop 3, in 2011: Sharing of guidelines, and recommended coping strategies; and a Final Conference: in 2012: General dissemination of the outcomes of the Action, to likely beneficiaries.

The Action Website is at http://sites.google.com/site/costis0801.

Peter K. Smith

Whitehead Building
Psychology Department
Goldsmiths
University of London
New Cross
SE14 6NW
UK
Tel. +44 20 7919 7898
Fax +44 20 7919 7873
E-mail p.smith@gold.ac.uk

EU Kids Online

Sonia Livingstone and Leslie Haddon
London School of Economics and Political Science, London, UK

EU Kids Online

Funded by the European Commission's Safer Internet Programme, EU Kids Online (2006–2009) is a thematic network that aimed to identify, compare, and draw conclusions from existing and ongoing research on children and online technologies conducted in Europe. Having constructed a publicly accessible and searchable database of nearly 400 studies conducted across Europe, it became clear that research is unevenly distributed across Europe, with most in Germany, the UK, and Denmark, and least in Cyprus, Bulgaria, Poland, Iceland, Slovenia, and Ireland. Although most countries strategically shape the research agenda through collaboration among universities, research councils, government ministries and, sometimes, industry, in countries where little research funding exists, the EC has significantly shaped the research agenda. In countries where Internet use is high, media coverage tends to focus the research agenda on risks and safety awareness.

Findings – Online Use and Risk

Children's use of the Internet continues to grow. Striking recent rises are evident among younger children, in countries which have recently entered the EU, and among parents, reversing the previous trend for teenagers especially to outstrip adults in Internet use. Long-standing gender inequalities may be disappearing, though socio-economic inequalities persist in most countries. Across Europe, despite some cross-national variation, available findings suggest that for online teenagers, the rank ordering of risks experienced is fairly similar. Giving out personal information is the most common risky behavior, followed by encountering pornography online, then by seeing violent or hateful content. Being bullied online comes fourth, followed by receiving unwanted sexual comments. Meeting an online contact offline appears the least common though arguably the most dangerous risk.

Even though higher status parents are more likely than those of lower status to provide their children with access to the Internet, it seems that the children from lower status homes are more exposed to risk online. There are also gender differences in risk, with boys more likely to encounter (or create) conduct risks and with girls more affected by content and contact risks. Countries were classified by degree of children's Internet use and degree of risk online. This suggests a positive correlation between use and risk: Northern European countries tend to be "high use, high risk"; Southern European countries tend to be "low use, low risk"; and Eastern European countries tend to be "new use, new risk".

Policy Recommendations – Maximizing Opportunities

E-inclusion policies should target countries where children's Internet use is relatively low (Italy, Greece, and Cyprus), along with certain population segments (less well-off households and parents who are not online) if the remaining 25% of EU children are to get online. Balancing empowerment and protection is crucial, since increasing online access and use tends to increase online risks; conversely, strategies to decrease risks can restrict children's online opportunities, possibly undermining children's rights or restricting their learning to cope with a degree of risk. Balancing these competing goals requires a mix of regulation, media literacy, and improved interface design. Positive online provision is also important: There are growing indications that such provision, if valued by children, directly benefits their development and reduces online risks by encouraging valuable and valued activities.

Greater Internet use is associated with higher levels of education, so educational achievement may be expected to increase the extent and sophistication of Internet use. Further, gaps in ICT provision and insufficient/outdated provision of ICT in schools should be addressed, and media education should be recognized and resourced as a core element of school curricula and infrastructure.

Policy Recommendations – Minimizing Risks

There are good grounds to strengthen regulatory frameworks across Europe, especially in some countries, since substantial proportions of children are encountering content, contact, and conduct risks, and since many children and parents lack the tools and skills by which they can prevent or manage such exposure. Self-regulatory provision in improving children's safety online is to be welcomed and supported, although it is not always transparent or independently evaluated. Children can only be supported in managing the online environment if this is substantially regulated – by law enforcement, interface and website design, search processes, content and service providers, online safety resources, etc. – just as they can only be taught to cross a road on which drivers and driving are carefully regulated.

Priorities for future awareness raising should concentrate on countries identified by research as high risk (Estonia, the Netherlands, Norway, Poland, Slovenia, and the UK); on countries which have rapidly and recently adopted the Internet, where access appears to exceed skills and cultural adjustment (Bulgaria, Estonia, Greece, Poland, and Portugal); and on countries where children's use exceeds parents' use (Hungary, Malta, Poland, and Romania). Awareness-raising priorities should focus on younger children; on strategies to encourage coping after exposure to risk; on addressing girls and boys differently; and on targeting less privileged families, schools, and neighborhoods. Awareness raising should encompass new risks as these emerge, especially on mobile platforms and via peer-to-peer content and services.

Policy must move beyond the division between child victims and adult perpetrators. Some children perpetrate online risks, whether from malice, playfulness, or mere accident; those who tend to experience online risks may generate further risks; those who create risks may also be victims; and those who are vulnerable online may lack adequate social support offline. Although no one doubts that parents are responsible for their children's safety, evidence suggests that they should not be relied upon as many are unaware or unable to mediate their children's online activities. Rules and restrictions do not fit well with the ethos of modern parenting, especially in some countries, and it is unclear that parental strategies are effective in reducing children's exposure to risk or increasing their resilience to cope.

Given the growing impetus behind media literacy initiatives, it is timely to evaluate their effectiveness in increasing children's critical knowledge of the online environment. The changing demands of a complex technological, commercial and, increasingly, user-generated environment sets limits on children's media literacy. Hence the importance of co- and self-regulation to support children's media literacy.

Research Recommendations

There are some significant gaps in the evidence base. Research priorities include:

- Younger children, especially in relation to risk and coping, though continually updated research on teenagers is also important.
- Emerging contents (especially "Web 2.0") and services (especially if accessed via mobile, gaming, or other platforms).
- Understanding children's developing skills of navigation and search, content interpretation, and critical evaluation.
- New and challenging risks, such as self-harm, suicide, pro-anorexia, drugs, hate/racism, gambling, addiction, illegal downloading, and commercial risks (sponsorship, embedded or viral marketing, use of personal data, and GPS tracking).
- How children (and parents) do and should respond to online risk.
- How to identify particularly vulnerable or "at risk" children within the general population.
- Evaluations of the effectiveness of technical solutions, parental mediation, media literacy, and other awareness and safety measures, both in terms of the ease of implementation and more importantly in terms of their impact on risk reduction; this may vary for different groups of children in different cultural contexts.

To advance this agenda, and since methods of researching children, the online environment, and countries in comparative perspective are all demanding, EU Kids Online produced two reports on methodology – a literature review and a best practice research guide, plus additional online resources to guide researchers (see below).

EU Kids Online II: Enhancing Knowledge Regarding European Children's Use, Risk, and Safety Online

EU Kids Online II is a new project funded by the EC Safer Internet Programme, designed to examine children's and parents' experiences and practices regarding use, risk, and safety online. This second project undertaken by the EU Kids Online network comprises some 70 experts in social uses of the Internet and new media, media education and digital literacy, childhood and family studies, the psychology of adolescence and identity, legal and regulatory perspectives, and research methods.

Between 2009 and 2011, EU Kids Online II will conduct original empirical research across member states with national samples of children aged 9–16 years and their parents. The aim is to produce a rigorous, cross-nationally comparative quantitative evidence base regarding Internet use across Europe. Directed by Professor Sonia Livingstone of the London School of Economics and Political Science, the project team includes a multinational management group, an international advisory panel, and research teams in over 20 participating countries across Europe.

Why is This Research Needed?

EU Kids Online I (2006–2009) examined available findings on cultural, contextual, and risk issues in children's use of online technologies across 21 countries and findings from 400+ studies, identifying key findings and pinpointing gaps in the evidence base. Its reports examine data availability, comparative findings, best research practice, research contexts, and policy recommendations. Online risks high on public, research, and policy agendas include exposure to inappropriate content (e.g., pornographic, self-harm and violent content, and racist/hate material), unwelcome contact (e.g., grooming, sexual harassment, bullying, and abuse of personal information and privacy), and attracting growing attention, inappropriate conduct by children themselves (e.g., bullying and abuse of privacy).

But exactly how common these risks are, how much risks result in genuine harm, how children react, whether some children are particularly vulnerable, how parents can or should act – all these questions and more await cross-nationally comparative and reliable research for their answers. Furthermore, it is important to avoid moral panics or exaggerated anxieties, particularly as these may result in efforts to constrain children's freedoms or limit their opportunities online.

Adopting an approach which is child centered, comparative, critical, and contextual, EU Kids Online II aims to design, conduct, and analyze a major quantitative survey of children's experiences of online risk. The survey will encompass questions about children's Internet use, digital literacy, coping responses, perceptions, and safety practices. These findings will be systematically compared to the perceptions and practices of their parents.

Specific Objectives

- To design a thorough and robust survey instrument appropriate for identifying the nature of children's online access, use, risk, coping, and safety awareness.
- To design a thorough and robust survey instrument appropriate for identifying the nature of parental experiences, practices, and concerns regarding their children's Internet use.
- To administer the survey in a reliable and ethically sensitive manner to national samples of Internet users aged 9–16, and their parents, in member states.
- To analyze the results systematically so as to identify both core findings and more complex patterns among findings on a national and comparative basis.
- To disseminate the findings in a timely manner to a wide range of relevant stakeholders nationally, across Europe, and internationally.
- To identify and disseminate key recommendations relevant to the development of safety awareness initiatives in Europe.

- To identify any remaining knowledge gaps and methodological lessons learned, to inform future projects regarding the promotion of safer use of the Internet and new online technologies.

Expected Results

- Core findings regarding children's and parents' experiences of online technologies, focused on comparisons of children's and parents' perceptions of and practices regarding online risk and safety.
- Patterns of risk and safety online to be identified following top-down hypothesis testing and bottom-up exploration of relationships among different variables, conducted on a cross-national basis.
- Evidence-based policy and research recommendations.

Timetable

Autumn 2009	Project planning, survey design, sampling
Spring 2010	Fieldwork
Summer 2010	Core data analysis
Autumn 2010	Report on core findings
Spring 2011	Contextual and comparative analysis
Summer 2011	Final report and recommendations

References

Livingstone, S., & Haddon, L. (Eds.). (2009). *Kids Online: Opportunities and risks for children*. Bristol: The Policy Press.

For all project reports and outputs, for network contacts, and for further information, see www.eukidsonline.net. Separate national reports are also available on the website. Project reports include the following:

de Haan, J., & Livingstone, S. (2009). *EU Kids Online: Policy and research recommendations*.

Hasebrink, U., Livingstone, S., & Haddon, L. (2008). *Comparing children's online opportunities and risks across Europe: Cross-national comparisons for EU Kids Online* (2nd ed., 2009).

Livingstone, S., & Haddon, L. (2009). *EU Kids Online: Final report*.

Lobe, B., Livingstone, S., & Haddon, L. (2007). *Researching children's experiences online across countries: Issues and problems in methodology*.

Lobe, B., Livingstone, S., Ólafsson, K., & Simões, J. (2008). *Best practice research guide: How to research children and online technologies in comparative perspective* (Available as a pdf and online FAQs).

Staksrud, E., Livingstone, S., & Haddon, L. (2007). *What do we know about children's use of online technologies? A report on data availability and research gaps in Europe* (2nd ed., 2009).

Stald, G., & Haddon, L. (2008). *Cross-cultural contexts of research: Factors influencing the study of children and the Internet in Europe*.

Sonia Livingstone

Department of Media and Communications
London School of Economics and Political Science
Houghton Street
London WC2A 2AE
UK
Tel. +44 20 7955 7710
Fax +44 20 7955 7248
E-mail s.livingstone@lse.ac.uk

Call for Papers

"Consumer Behavior and Economic Decisions"

A Topical Issue of the *Zeitschrift für Psychologie / Journal of Psychology*

Guest Editors: Erich Kirchler and Erik Hölzl (University of Vienna, Austria)

Consumer behavior and economic decisions are an applied field of research informed by several disciplines, for example, psychology, economics, marketing, and also by several subdisciplines in psychology, for example, general, social, or economic psychology. The focus on decisions provides a framework to integrate these perspectives. Decision research can provide several promising approaches for the understanding of consumer behavior, for example, by distinguishing between impulsive and extensive decisions or between automatic, affective, and cognitive routes to decisions.

This Special Issue invites submissions of empirical and theoretical papers on consumer behavior and economic decisions, with a particular focus on decision processes. The purpose of this Special Issue is to highlight recent research and innovative approaches. Papers that focus on the following topics are particularly welcome:

- spending decisions
- saving decisions
- credit use decisions
- insurance and pension plan decisions
- investment decisions (stocks and bonds)
- money management decisions.

We invite researchers to submit contributions electronically to Erich Kirchler (erich.kirchler@univie.ac.at) and Erik Hölzl (erik.hoelzl@univie.ac.at).

There is a *two-stage submission process*. Initially, authors are requested to submit only abstracts of their proposed papers. All proposals will be subject to editorial review. Authors requested to submit full papers should then do so. All papers will undergo full peer review.

Deadline for submission of abstracts is April 15, 2010.
Deadline for submission of full papers is August 15, 2010.

The journal seeks to maintain a short turnaround time, with the final version of the accepted papers being due by January 15, 2011. The topical issue will be published as Issue 4 (2011).

The *Zeitschrift für Psychologie / Journal of Psychology* was founded in 1890 and is the second oldest psychology journal in the world. One of the founding Editors was Hermann Ebbinghaus. Since 2007, it has been published in English and has been devoted to publishing topical issues that provide state-of-the-art reviews of current research in psychology.

Guidelines for article preparation:

- only English-language submissions can be considered;
- contributions must be original (not published previously or currently under review for publication elsewhere);
- regular articles should not exceed 45,000 characters and spaces in length, including references, figures, and tables (allowances for figures and tables should be deducted on the basis of size – ~ 1,250 characters for a quarter-page figure/table);
- other submission formats (research summaries, opinion pieces, etc.) may be considered, please contact the Editors for details;
- reference citations in the text and in the reference list should be in accordance with the principles set out in the Publication Manual of the American Psychological Association (5th ed.) – see also any recent issue of the journal;
- submissions should be typeset in a standard font such as Times/Times New Roman 12 pt, with a margin of 3 cm;
- illustrations and tables must be submitted on a separate page.

For detailed author guidelines, please see the journal's website at www.hogrefe.com/journals/zfp/.

DOI: 10.1027/0044-3409.217.4.240

Volume Information

Volume 217, 2009

Table of Contents

Topical Issue: Beyond the Significance Test Ritual

Topical Issue: Becoming a Science: A Historical Perspective on Pioneering Work in Psychology

Topical Issue: New Directions in Multinomial Modeling

Topical Issue: Cyberbullying: Abusive Relationships in Cyberspace

DOI: 10.1027/0044-3409-217.4.241

Research Spotlight

Opinion

Horizons

Calls for Papers

Volume Information, Volume 217, 2009

Author Index

Keyword Index

Reviewers 2009

The *Zeitschrift für Psychologie / Journal of Psychology* expresses its thanks to the following colleagues who contributed to the peer review of manuscripts this year. They reviewed the incoming manuscripts very conscientiously and provided constructive suggestions to many of our authors. Furthermore, in most cases they reviewed quickly, which is a fundamental prerequisite for a rapid manuscript management. The editors of the *Zeitschrift für Psychologie / Journal of Psychology* are greatly indebted to all of them.

Sheri Bauman
Ute Bayen
Frank Bellezza
Elfriede Billmann-Mahecha
AntonellaBrighi
Arndt Bröder
Axel Buchner
Thomas Chesney
Geoffrey Cumming
Gie Deboutte
Julian Dooley
Edgar Erdfelder
Fiona Fidler
Klaus Foppa
Ann Frisen
Andrew Gelman
Jeff Gill
Pablo Gomez
Vasiliki Gountsidou
Tali Heiman
Caterina Katzer
Peter Killeen
Jette Kofoed
James T. Lamiell
Lothar Laux
Qing Li
Geoffrey Loftus
Helmut E. Lück
Eric Maris
Robert R. McCrae
Ersilia Menesini
Stephen Minton
Joaquin Mora-Merchan
Jochen Musch
Natalie Noret
Jacek Pyzalski
Michel Regenwetter
Helmut Reich
David Riefer
Robert Rosenthal
Ralph Rosnow
Ralf Rummer
Anna Sevcikova
Phillip Slee
David Spiegelhalter
Dalene Stangl
Georges Steffgen
Dagmar Strohmeier
Neil Tippett
Francis Tuerlinckx
Heidi Vandebosch
Manuel Voelkle
Howard Wainer
Rainer Westermann
Uwe Wolfradt

